:S IN BRITISH FOREIGN POLICY,

ritish Consuls since 1825
I TRADE 1806–1914
1930: An Inquiry based on British Experience

NENTAL EUROPE AND THE USA,

ND CANADA: Studies in Comparative
or with Guido di Tella*)
' OF ARGENTINA, 1880–1946 (*editor with Guido*

)VERSEAS ON THE EVE OF THE FIRST
d Abuse of Numbers
1950: Australia, Argentina and Canada Compared

in

Also by D. C. M. Platt

FINANCE, TRADE AND POLIT
1815–1914
THE CINDERELLA SERVICE:
LATIN AMERICA AND BRITI
BUSINESS IMPERIALISM, 184
in Latin America (*editor*)
FOREIGN FINANCE IN CON
1815–1870
*ARGENTINA, AUSTRALIA
Development, 1870–1965 (*ed*
*THE POLITICAL ECONOM
di Tella)
*BRITAIN'S INVESTMENT
WORLD WAR: The Use
*SOCIAL WELFARE, 1850
(*editor*)

**Also published by Macmil*

Mickey Mouse Numbers in World History

The Short View

D. C. M. Platt
Professor of the History of Latin America
University of Oxford

M
MACMILLAN
PRESS

First published 1989

Published by
THE MACMILLAN PRESS LTD
Houndmills, Basingstoke, Hampshire RG21 2XS
and London
Companies and representatives
throughout the world

Printed in Hong Kong

British Library Cataloguing in Publication Data
Platt, D.C.M. (Desmond Christopher St. Martin)
1934–
Mickey Mouse numbers in world history.
1. History–Statistical Methods
I. Title
902.8
ISBN 0–333–46787–6

Keep well the Hermetic Decalogue,
   which runs as follows:

Thou shalt not do as the dean pleases.
Thou shall not write thy doctor's thesis
   On education.
Thou shall not worship projects nor
Shalt thou or thine bow down before
   Administration.

Thou shalt not answer questionnaires
Or quizzes upon World-Affairs,
   Nor with compliance
Take any test. Thou shalt not sit
With statisticians nor commit
   a social science.

Thou shalt not live within thy means
Nor on plain water and raw greens.
   If thou must choose
Between the chances, choose the odd:
Read *The New Yorker*, trust in God;
   And take short views.

W. H. Auden, *Under Which Lyre: A Reactionary Tract for the Times* (Phi Beta Kappa Poem, Harvard, 1946)

Contents

Preface and Acknowledgements

This book, like Latin in the professor's opening lecture, is 'the relentless foe of woolly minds'. The point is that thoughts and mistakes of one generation lead too easily to the conclusions of another. A Victorian encyclopedist finds an admirer in a Nobel Laureate (1971); a second Laureate (1974) quotes the first; a third (1977) and a fourth (1979) quote all and sundry; 'development historians' take their conclusions from the wilder shores of 'world' historical demography. This has often proved difficult to trace. I have tried my best. An asterisk (*) before names indicates that the approach to numbers is questioned in the text; **bold** numbers in the index proclaim the precise spot.

I owe much to my students, friends and colleagues in Oxford and elsewhere. I am grateful, as ever, to my wife Sylvia for her constant help and support, and to my friend Stephen Cohn for suggesting the perfect epigraph. Above all, I am indebted to those great libraries known collectively as the Bodleian – 'those arsenals of divine vengeance', in A. E. Housman's happy phrase.

The epigraph, from Edward Mendelson (ed.), *W. H. Auden: Collected Poems*, is reprinted by kind permission of Faber & Faber Ltd and Random House, Inc.

St Antony's College
Oxford

D. C. M. PLATT

Introduction

If there is one central theme that runs throughout this book it is that poor numbers are bad not only in themselves but because, more damagingly, they encourage unreliable conclusions. Of course, they can still prove useful if guided and directed by sound scholarship and reason. Alexander Gerschenkron, in his review of *Simon Kuznets's *Income and Wealth*, explained that if calculations from quantitative data 'are at variance with what we should expect from general historical knowledge, they should be rejected'.[1] He was asking no more than we expect from our pocket calculators: the illuminated display is checked against common sense.

I am not pretending that I can myself supply better numbers for most of the *bêtises* I describe; the evidence has vanished if it ever existed, and may never be discovered. All that I can say is that over a very wide area – 'world history', no less – existing conventional derivations are open to doubt. We move among many and endure the extremes – amateurs and enthusiasts, encyclopedists, bureaucrats, 'number-crunchers', cliometricians and political visionaries. We are dealing, after all, with Fernand Braudel's *longue durée*.

Much has happened in the two centuries since numbers have come to be hoarded, cherished and reproduced. I shall try to identify the main elements, the stages, and the fallacies, in the hope that I may at least encourage a proper spirit of caution and doubt. A younger *Colin Clark, when about to exchange academic speculation for the realities of government service, assured us that theory had a 'valuable, indeed an essential part to play in the development of economic science'. But, as he said, 'it must be theory which respects facts, not tries to supersede them'.[2]

It may simply be a difference of approach. In the most primitive terms the economist seeks first to create a 'model' and only then to confirm it from the evidence; the historian, ideally, looks first at the evidence from which he only then derives conclusions - all of which was explained more subtly in a friendly engagement between Robert Fogel and Sir Geoffrey Elton.[3]

The range of accessible evidence has increased hugely since Carlyle's day when history was 'the essence of innumerable biographies'. But it is true that the better information of today has created a serious problem for 'world' history. Bad data, A. G.

Hopkins explains, 'sustain simple theories of a complex world; good data inhibit generalisation'.[4] *Braudel was magnificent on the Mediterranean in the sixteenth century, where the numbers were sparse; he was less impressive as he approached the present day. Even now we may not in practice have so much 'good' data; my target is generalisation from 'bad' data. Hopkins has put his finger on it: 'good data', if we had such things, would certainly 'inhibit generalisation'.

In the first sentence of his *Objectivity in Social Research*, *Gunnar Myrdal declared roundly that 'the ethos of social science is the search for "objective" truth'.[5] Modern number-gatherers warn us, quite rightly, that even if statistics are useful in historical studies, they should not be employed carelessly and casually in 'comparisons over time and between countries':

> Let the users of this volume [*B. R. Mitchell's *European Historical Statistics 1750–1970*] be in no doubt of the need to seek for subtlety and of the difficulties in the way of precision.[6]

But then, as *Paul Bairoch, a well-known handler of world statistics, once explained: 'to omit all statistics containing a margin of error would amount to renouncing any attempt at economic analysis';[7] and it is true that books such as his could not have been written at all. The simple question is whether, if the conclusions derived from inaccurate statistics are wrong-headed, Bairoch's *The Economic Development of the Third World since 1900* should have found a Paris publisher in 1967, been translated by Cynthia Postan, and then republished in London in 1975? Should its figures have supplied the basis for much teaching and generalisation ever since?

'It is undesirable to believe a proposition when there is no ground whatever for supposing it true' (Bertrand Russell, 1928). If we are lucky, errors may cancel each other out. But they may also proliferate. Charles Kindleberger, in an apologetic preface to his first 'empirical study of monographic length' (1956), found consolation in the notion that although any results of his research into the terms of trade might be 'worthless or harmful, the cumulative effect of many attempts, so runs the scientific faith, may lead to meaningful results'.[8] Kindleberger may now be less inclined to subscribe, even in jest, to the 'scientific faith'. But what I hope to establish in the investigation that follows is that time and again these 'many attempts', although superficially the outcome of an individual's research, draw simply on a single and unconvincing source. One example could be a fundamental figure for 'world' trade, invented by a Victorian statistical fantasist, which then reappears in the equations of today's econometricians; another could be an estimate of the different elements in the 'world's' population, composed in a Leipzig study in the 1890s, which, via the *League of Nations/United Nations, became the basis for generalisations on the deterioration in per capita distribution of wealth between the First and Third Worlds in the 1980s.

Generalisation is indeed the trouble. Kindleberger, an honest guide, found that his researches on terms of trade between countries revealed simply that there were as many terms of trade as there were pairs of countries. He had been struck, in his intrusion (as an economist) into empiricism, 'by the frequency with which indexes are launched on an unsuspecting world without an adequate account of their genealogy'.[9] *Paul Lamartine Yates explained that the absence of any serious breakdown into commodity groups meant that 'statistical series purporting to show changes in quantum and unit prices of manufactures, primary products and other such groups rest on particularly slim bases'; often they represented little more than the data from two or three exporting/importing countries. Yates himself declared that he had supplied merely a 'handbook' of possibly useful statistics; he had deliberately held aloof from the elaboration of theories, for the most part resisting 'the temptation to suggest what the figures signify'.[10]

It was a temptation that many, like *Sir Arthur Lewis, have failed to resist, and Yates has proved the source for much mistaken generalisation. The danger lies with those who have calmly taken bogus statistics in the simple faith that they are accurate, and then employed them to construct great theories. It lies too with those who have blandly republished the figures as gigantic 'data banks' from which, in time, information is generously and unquestioningly extracted – and I mean professionals such as *Deane and *Mitchell quite apart from lesser anthologists like *Mulhall, *Maddison and *Woodruff.

Statistics, by the early decades of the nineteenth century, had become something of an obsession with a dedicated minority. The Statistical Society of London (later the Royal Statistical Society) was founded in 1834. It followed a French model and was itself imitated throughout Britain and, indeed, all over the world. The British Association for the Advancement of Science (Dickens's 'Mud-Fog Association for the Advancement of Everything') followed in the same vein. Although the first attempts – the squirrel's gathering and storing of every scrap of unascribed numbers – were notably amateurish, the quality improved. Censuses and annual trade statistics, whatever their failings, were characteristic of European and European-derived countries by the second half of the century, so that one of the leading nations in statistics in the years before the First World War was, in fact, Argentina.

There are obvious limits. It was not until the 1930s, largely inspired by Keynes, that economists became aware of the importance of national income statistics. Yet it is from this that 'real income per capita' became so critical a calculation among 'development historians', projected back even into the mid-nineteenth century.[11] And it is, or should be, chastening to find a professor of monetary economics at the University of Rome who in 1987, while challenging the 'Italian Miracle', reminds us that national income statistics are *still* 'very difficult to take at face valuation'.[12] This might suggest that the statistics for Europe's gross national product from 1800, in *Bairoch,[13] take some stomaching, let alone *Maizel's GDP for 'selected countries' (including Argentina) from 1899,[14] *Kuznets's net national product for France from 1831 to 1840 and a GDP for Japan from 1874 to 1949,[15] or *Maddison's GDP for a whole range of countries before 1914 including France and Britain from 1700, 'Germany' from 1820, and Japan from 1870.[16]

It is all reminiscent of those estimates for 'national wealth' calculated so assiduously by patriots from the middle of the nineteenth century. Sir Josiah Stamp, first Baron Stamp (1880–1941), government statistician and *éminence grise*, took a hand in such improbable exercises, although 'devoted to the pursuit of academic scholarship' (*Dictionary of National Biography*). The statistics for foreign trade are more reliable, for reasons to which I shall return, but the problem has always been the incompatibility of data. Even for the years after the Second World War, Allen and Ely have found that although British and European dependencies have shared the characteristics of the imperial power, and Latin American trade statistics have tended to have similar features, it is difficult to find many common threads in the methods of countries in that huge area, the Near and Far East.[17]

In practice, the figures computed for 'world' trade before 1914 were for Europe and its colonies, for the Americas, China and Japan; the *League of Nations certainly worked on that assumption in *Folke Hilgerdt's *Industrialisation and Foreign Trade* (Geneva, 1945). The result has been a tendency to underestimate those domestic activities that took forms unrecorded in European-style government statistics. But 'Europeanised' trade statistics, quite apart from the noticeable division that exists between 'Anglo-Saxon' and 'Continental' method, are difficult to use, and it is as well to remember it. The accuracy of these statistics is an area which is not directly relevant to the issues I discuss. The problems have often been described: different valuations ('official'/'declared' values), definitions (widely at variance before the Brussels classification of 1913), origins and destinations, fiscal and calendar years. As the League of Nations put it, the accuracy of foreign trade statistics in its own publications depended ultimately on the information supplied by the mercantile community,[18] while the manner in which trade returns were drawn up 'differed greatly from country to country, and sometimes from year to year'.[19] I have quoted elsewhere[20] the views of a committee of the British Association, published with the report of its annual meeting of 1904. The committee's members included the foremost statisticians of the day, A. L. Bowley, Professor S. J. Chapman and Sir Robert Giffen, and they were asked to enquire into the accuracy and comparability of British and foreign statistics for international trade. The committee could find no case where the values registered by country X of goods imported from country Y corresponded at all closely with the values registered by Y as exported to X:

> In most countries the statistics are compiled first in that way which is most useful for their fiscal purposes, and secondarily in such a way as to give information to their own people. No two countries are in quite similar commercial situations, or have identical fiscal policies, and the non-comparability of statistics naturally results. The most perfectly accurate statistics readily lead to inaccurate deductions, when their origin, nature and limitations are not thoroughly understood.[21]

Government statistics regularly reflect government policy – they are 'affected by a nation's belief as to how the information may be used to its own advantage or disadvantage'.[22] But private statistics can be as bad; they too can reflect the prejudices of the compiler. *Stephen Bourne, in his maturity, became an active member of London's Statistical Society and an extreme propagandist for free trade. His collected works in *Trade, Population and Food: A Series of Papers on Economic Statistics* (1880) used doubtful numbers to advance a strongly felt case; he was partisan to a degree and took the figures that suited his argument. *J. E. Cairnes was a strong opponent of protection and an advocate of *laissez-faire* and free trade; his figures in *Some Leading Principles of Political Economy* (London, 1874) reflect his views. Again, *Michael Mulhall was an ardent free trader. In the fourth and final edition of his *Dictionary of Statistics* (London, 1899) he discovered a huge increase in 'world' trade, no less than 80 per cent in the 1850s, 'that period being contemporaneous with the introduction of free trade'.

Ironically, the estimates for the stock of Britain's investment overseas just before the First World War were inflated by free traders and fair traders alike; it happened that both arguments (in the debate on tariff reform) profited from a high figure, and a high figure it became.[23] For the world generally, Grover Clark's *Balance Sheets of Imperialism*, cited frequently as a source-book for figures, was published in association with his anti-empire tract *A Place in the Sun*. Clark's heartfelt and emotional intention was to identify what he called the 'debit entries which must be made in the ledger of imperialism'; not unexpectedly, he derived from his assortment of figures the conviction that the arguments for holding colonies were fallacious.[24] All that *Jacob Viner could discover from Raúl Prebisch's *Economic Development of Latin America and its Principal Problems* (United Nations: New York, 1949), and from the related literature, was 'the dogmatic identification of agriculture with poverty'. Viner found their 'natural laws' for the most part to be but 'mischievous fantasies'.[25]

Essentially, what is wanted by both bureaucrats and propagandists is *some* figure, *any* figure, to lead off a series, after which gains and losses can be assessed over the *longue durée*. Cliometricians discover the same need in the construction of models and giant equations. I will return to this later, and in greater detail, and it may be enough at present to call attention to Britain's *Key Statistics*, published by *The Times* and prepared under the patronage of the London and Cambridge Economic Service (1966). *Key Statistics* makes sensible use (after 1918) of British government statistics such as those from the *Board of Trade Journal*. Nonetheless (and characteristically for this genre of statistical compendia) it feels the need to start off with mysterious figures, if only to introduce the better figures that follow. In Table N ('external finance, world trade and production') we are offered a United Kingdom share for 1899 and 1913 of 33.2 per cent and 30.2 per cent respectively (the exports of manufactures from eleven industrial countries); we are given, simultaneously, an index number (average 1958 = 100) for 'Industrial countries (OECD including Japan)' of 23 in 1899 and 28 in 1911.[26] Although unfootnoted, the first came from Board of Trade numbers, and the second from the *League of Nations. 'Official' figures appeal to official minds. . . .

Perhaps this is unimportant. One has to start somewhere, after all, if only to complete an otherwise ragged table. A number can be convenient merely as a backdrop. If all that is wanted is an indication of great size, it hardly matters whether, say, the stock of British investment overseas at the outbreak of the First World War was £4 billion or £3 billion. The trouble starts at the next level, when it might be more to the point to discover the direction in which that investment travelled, or the effect that it might have had on the shape of British and foreign economies.[27] It is not a parochial matter. In 'world history', as I hope to explain, the problem arises when 'world' numbers are taken to illustrate some gigantic trend.

Notes

1. Alexander Gerschenkron, *Economic Backwardness in Historical Perspective: A Book of Essays* (New York, 1962) p. 438.
2. Colin Clark, *The Conditions of Economic Progress* (London, 1940) p. viii.
3. Robert William Fogel and G. R. Elton, *Which Road to the Past?: Two Views of History* (New Haven, Conn., 1983) p. 75.
4. A. G. Hopkins, 'Big Business in African Studies', *Journal of African History*, 28:1 (1987) p. 130.
5. Gunnar Myrdal, *Objectivity in Social Research* (London, 1970) p. 3.
6. B. R. Mitchell, *European Historical Statistics 1750–1970* (London, 1975) pp. viii and ix.
7. Paul Bairoch, *The Economic Development of the Third World since 1900* (trans. edn London, 1975) p. 4.
8. Charles P. Kindleberger, *The Terms of Trade: A European Case Study* (New York, 1956) p. 11.
9. *Ibid.*, p. v.
10. P. Lamartine Yates, *Forty Years of Foreign Trade* (London, 1959) p. 19.
11. For example, by *L. J. Zimmerman, 'The Distribution of World Income 1860–1900', in E. DeVries (ed.), *Essays on Unbalanced Growth* (The Hague, 1962).

12. Antonio Martino, 'An Italian Miracle? Don't Bank on It', *The Times*, 9 February 1987.
13. Paul Bairoch, 'Europe's Gross National Product: 1800–1975', *Journal of European Economic History*, 5:2 (Autumn, 1976).
14. Alfred Maizels, *Industrial Growth and World Trade: An Empirical Study of Trends in Production, Consumption and Trade from 1899–1955* (Cambridge, 1963) p. 531.
15. Simon Kuznets, *Economic Growth of Nations; Total Output and Production Structures* (Cambridge, Mass., 1971) pp. 11 and 13.
16. Angus Maddison, *Phases of Capitalist Development* (Oxford, 1982) Appendix A.
17. R. G. D. Allen and J. Edward Ely (eds), *International Trade Statistics* (New York, 1953) p. 5.
18. League of Nations, *Memorandum on Balance of Payments and Foreign Trade Balances 1910–23*, Vol. II, *Trade Statistics of Forty-Two Countries* (Geneva, 1924) p. 11.
19. *Ibid.*, Vol. I, *Balance of Payments and Summary Trade Tables*, p. 41. These two volumes (notes 18 and 19) contain the basic explanation of the League's methodology in international trade statistics for all subsequent issues.
20. D. C. M. Platt, 'Problems in the Interpretation of Foreign Trade Statistics before 1914', *Journal of Latin American Studies*, 3:2 (1971) p. 130.
21. British Association for the Advancement of Science, *Annual Report for 1904* (London, 1905) pp. 309–10.
22. Allen and Ely, *International Trade Statistics*, p. 3.
23. D. C. M. Platt, *Britain's Investment Overseas on the Eve of the First World War: The Use and Abuse of Numbers* (London, 1986) pp. 68–71.
24. Grover Clark, *The Balance Sheets of Imperialism: Facts and Figures on Colonies* (New York, 1936) pp. 3, 11–17. A modern attempt at quantifying the gains and losses of imperialism has again come to grief on rocky data.
25. Jacob Viner, *International Trade and Economic Development* (Oxford, 1953) p. 44.
26. The London and Cambridge Economic Service, *The British Economy: Key Statistics 1900–1966* (London, n.d.) p. 17.
27. I apologise for returning to an obsession; the argument is in my *Britain's Investment Overseas*, cited above (note 23). Indeed, I must confess to having done as much myself when, in more innocent days, I employed a whole table from the hapless Rippy merely to establish the obvious point that British investment in Latin America, 1880–1913, was large and growing (*Latin America and British Trade*, London, 1972, p. 289). I hope that I am not myself now quoted as having given authority to those odd figures!

Part I
The Sowers

1 The Recorders

I have referred to a commonly-felt need for numbers which date back before the First World War, simply as a start to modern statistical series. The problem now is to identify the sources.

THE FIRST GENERATION: PORTER, McCULLOCH AND MACGREGOR

George Richardson Porter (1792–1852), a failed sugar broker who subsequently 'devoted himself to economics and statistics' (*Dictionary of National Biography*), was a founder in 1834 of London's Statistical Society. He took an active interest in Section F (statistics) of the British Association. He was a zealous free trader. In 1834 he became the first chief of the Statistical Department of Britain's Board of Trade, and was then promoted to the joint secretaryship vacated by *John Macgregor.

British trade statistics, in their first comprehensible form, are still known as *Porter's Tables*, and it was during Porter's service with the Board of Trade that he published, first in 1836–8, then in 1846 and finally in 1851, the work for which he was (and is) best known: *The Progress of the Nation in its Various Social and Economical Relations, from the Beginning of the Nineteenth Century to the Present Time*. It is described by the *Dictionary of National Biography* as 'an invaluable record of the first half of the nineteenth century . . . remarkable for the accuracy and the variety of its information, and for the skill with which the results of statistical enquiry are presented'.

*F. W. Hirst, editor of *The Economist*, who as late as 1912 brought out a completely revised and updated edition of *The Progress of the Nation*, explained that Porter's first version was begun 'before the modern passion for government statistics had been developed or catered for', even if Porter's position in the Board of Trade had given him special access to information. In Hirst's opinion (and Hirst was a reliable guide), Porter's work, prejudiced as it was by its dogmatic propagandising of free trade, was nevertheless a 'storehouse of information, highly valued by all those who take a serious interest in the economic history of our country'.[1]

Porter's preoccupation was with Britain's domestic economy –

agriculture, manufacturing, population, internal communications and trade, public revenue and expenditure, consumption, accumulation, and moral progress. It was only in the very last part of his text that he considered the 'extent and condition of our colonies and foreign dependencies'.[2] In the present context it is this last part that is of interest; furthermore, Porter included three chapters on 'foreign' trade (based on Britain's government statistics for exports from 1827), British returns for shipping, and the official returns (trade and shipping) for France and the United States. His Section VIII (British colonies and dependencies) was taken, naturally, from 'British official figures', otherwise unspecified, and was a useful assembly of whatever statistical knowledge could be gathered by 1850 for British territory in each area of the world: Europe (Gibraltar, Malta, Heligoland and the Ionian Islands); Asia (India, Ceylon and Mauritius); Australasia; Canada; Africa (Sierra Leone, the Gold Coast, Fernando Po, South Africa and St. Helena).

Hirst and his collaborators (his staff on *The Economist*) thoroughly revised and updated Porter's British material. They included what by then (just before the First World War) had become an obligatory exercise, namely a chapter on the growth of national wealth and capital (with estimates for British capital since 1600!). Hirst took his updated figures very largely from British official sources, 'carefully tested and revised'.[3] But he abandoned Porter's section on 'Colonies and Dependencies' which, as he explained, would have required another volume for adequate treatment, and he omitted other countries except where appearing (unreferenced) in the main text. Hirst's edition, although a valuable handbook of the figures for Britain's social and economic development, was of even less value and interest to 'world' history than Porter's originals.

John Ramsay McCulloch (1789–1864), statistician and political economist, was Comptroller of Her Majesty's Stationery Office for a quarter of a century. His *Dictionary, Practical, Theoretical, and Historical, of Commerce and Commercial Navigation*, first published in 1832, was revised and improved in 1834 and 1844 and supplied with many supplements. It was what it claimed to be – a 'dictionary', intended for the use of British businessmen, but not impressive outside the range required: Buenos Aires (the port) was listed, but not Argentina (the Republic); Montevideo, but not Uruguay; Vera Cruz, but not Mexico . . . The longer entries were 'Insurance (principles of)' followed by 'Interest and Annuities'. Its value as a statistical record outside Britain is limited.

However, *John Macgregor (1797–1857)* promised more. His career was less distinguished: he absconded shortly before the collapse of his Royal British Bank and died in Boulogne. Macgregor, Fellow of the London Statistical Society and author of *British America* (for which he had travelled extensively in the 1830s gathering statistics), was a statistician in the traditional mould. His *Resources and Statistics of Nations* (London, 1834) included 'Geographical Position and Natural Resources, Area and Population, Political Statistics, Moral Statistics, Medical Statistics and Economical Statistics'. For Macgregor 'the science of statistics [was] that of *truth*', and he set himself the task of exhibiting the '*resources* and *statistics* of all nations'. From these he evolved generalisations, among which was the thought that because the climate of India was so oppressive, Europeans were carried about in palanquins by native Indians:

> Hence must appear the very feeble moral energy of the Natives, or, at least their want of will and judgement, to combine and direct their physical strength, in comparison with the mental power and ability of the Europeans who rule over them.[4]

Macgregor supplied figures for the mass of the world (Europe, Africa, Asia and the Americas) – the square mileage and population of China and its capital, Peking, the same for the Khanates of 'Boucharia' and Khiva and the Immanates of Yemen and 'Mascate', their revenues, and the size of their armies. Macgregor's Asian figures came from a Mr Balbi of Venice, the late M. Malte-Brün, and British *Parliamentary Papers*. But he had a mind of his own. Adam Smith was 'the ablest, and father, of them all', but even Smith 'had advanced some "*doctrines*" which had been falsified over the last fifty years', and the same applied to the 'otherwise invaluable works' of Ricardo, *McCulloch and Mill. In M. Say's 'admirable writings . . . we also discover *theories*, which subsequent enquiry has disproved'.[5] Only Oceania defeated him. Macgregor's 'materials' were 'easily related', viz:

> In Australia, the inhabitants are living in the most brutal state; the savages of Haraforas, in Borneo, and of the Molaccas are equally degraded . . . In all, priests and magistrates exercise frightful influence, and, in all, barbarism, anarchy, and, consequently, insecurity prevails.[6]

When Macgregor became Joint-Secretary to the Board of Trade (1840) he could draw on a mass of information, and he encouraged the collection of more. The five volumes of his *Commercial Statistics: A Digest of the Productive Resources etc. of All Nations* (London, 1844–50) are an immense improvement on his *Resources and Statistics* – more professional in every way. As he said in the preface to the first volume of *Commercial Statistics*, it was a kind of commercial dictionary, like the work which in England had been 'ably supplied by *Mr MacCulloch'. Most of his material – commercial tariffs, regulations and statistics of Europe and America – was gathered for the preparation of parliamentary returns.

Inevitably, Macgregor's *Commercial Statistics* fall short of what one might nowadays expect. Volumes I and II (1844) gave the figures, sometimes of reasonable quality, for Continental Europe. But they also included the 'statistics' of the 'Ottoman Empire' and 'African States' (by which he meant the *Arab* states). The population statistics, he admitted, 'appear exceedingly vague' and the 'absence of official returns, the internal dissensions, and the plague, cholera, etc. leave us no data on which we can rely with confidence'.[7] Volume III covered the United States and an imaginative slice of Spanish America from Mexico to Patagonia, drawn largely from such 'facts' and 'official' statistics as British diplomats and consular officers had been able to obtain. Volume IV published figures for Haiti, the non-British Indies (East and West), Brazil and Ceylon. The last, Volume V, took up the remainder: the Chinese Empire, British Possessions, UK trade and a host of random supplements. It was a Tradescantian 'Cabinet of Curiosities'.

MICHAEL G. MULHALL

Mulhall (1836–1900) owed much to the earlier generation, more particularly to *Macgregor. However, it is Mulhall who has attracted the most interest among 'world' historians, and he was right in claiming to have been the first actually to have produced and published a statistical 'dictionary' *tout court*. Every science to date, he explained, had had its own 'dictionary', except statistics, which was 'one of the reasons, perhaps, why so many philosophers deny this branch of study to be a science'.[8] Yet there was nothing 'scientific' about Mulhall. The epigraph to Mulhall's first *Dictionary* promised more than could be expected from such a work: 'Je n'impose rien, je ne propose même rien; j'expose.'

Mulhall was founding editor of the *Standard* (1861), an English-language newspaper in Buenos Aires, then hardly more than a large town. It was in Argentina that he first practised his life's passion, statistics. Mulhall's *Handbook of the River Plate* was published in several editions up to 1892. Meanwhile, he himself had returned to Britain, joined the London Statistical Society, and begun a career as self-appointed statistician-in-chief to the world. Mulhall's *Progress of the World: in Arts, Agriculture, Commerce, Manufactures, Instruction, Railways, and Public Wealth since the Beginning of the Nineteenth Century*, self-consciously an echo of *Porter's *Progress of the Nation*, was published in London in 1880. It was dedicated to 'the Press of Great Britain', for whom its nuggets of random information may occasionally have been useful. Subsequently, Mulhall produced a short book under the title *Balance Sheet of the World for the Ten Years 1870–1880* (London, 1881).

Economic historians know Mulhall primarily for his *Dictionary of Statistics*, the first edition of which was published in 1884 and the last (the fourth) in 1899. The figures were taken into the twentieth century by *Augustus Webb in his *New Dictionary of Statistics: A Complement to the Fourth Edition of Mulhall's Dictionary of Statistics* (London, 1911). Mulhall's *Industries and Wealth of Nations* (London, 1886) is also much cited in footnotes and bibliographies.

It may be as well to pass over the follies of Mulhall's *The English in South America* (Buenos Aires, 1878) – the first of his cornucopiae of miscellaneous, unverified/unverifiable information. *The English in South America* is a rag-bag of 'historical facts', dedicated primarily to the rôle of British mercenaries and adventurers during the struggle for independence. Yet it also contains such improbabilities as full figures (1877) for the population, revenue and trade of *all* the republics of South America and the empire of Brazil.

Mulhall's *Progress of the World* (1880) stepped up the search for miscellaneous 'facts': Holland's fishing in the Zuyder Zee ranged from 16 to 20 million herrings annually; there were 77.7 million sheep and hogs in the River Plate area . . . [9] More oddly still, although seductive for the catholic researcher into 'world' historical data, Mulhall supplied a figure for 'national expenditure' by the frail and undocumented republics of South America in 1820. The amount was £2 million, which worked out, he assured us, at three shillings per (unverified) inhabitant. By contrast, 'national expenditure' for

China and Japan in 1820 was £54.5 million, which could also be worked out at the (even less verifiable) figure of three shillings per inhabitant![10]

Mulhall seldom felt the need to cite his sources, in which he followed merely the practice of his contemporaries. In his *Balance Sheet of the World for the Ten Years 1870–1880* he found that the aggregate industries of South America had increased by 12 per cent (1870–1878), which meant 151 shillings per inhabitant in 1870, rising to 168 shillings in 1878.[11] The figures are utterly inexplicable. What were the 'aggregate industries of South America', how did one measure them, and who, in 1870, could provide reliable data for population?

The quality of Mulhall's *Dictionaries* improved, although the *Scotsman* had already welcomed the first edition of 1884 as being 'as trustworthy as it is unique', while the *Mark Lane Gazette* found it 'the model of a statistical work'.[12] Contemporaries were certainly impressed, although it is surprising to find Mulhall still cited a century later. Even the last edition of the *Dictionary* is, in the vocabulary of modern social 'science', 'deeply flawed'. For the third edition, possibly the best, Mulhall was able to list no less than 400 'books of reference' among which, unfortunately, there was no distinction of value, reliability or application; some were undoubtedly valuable, like the *Banker's Magazine* from 1844 to 1889 or *The Economist* from 1843 to 1890, while others, like *Stephen Bourne's *Population and Food*, are much less impressive.

Mulhall added another 140 bibliographical entries to his fourth edition. They included such treasures as Ozenne's *Statistical Atlas* (Paris, 1878) and J. Meusel's *Manual of Statistics*, published in Leipzig in 1782. The third edition of Mulhall's *Dictionary* comprised 'all known statistical data from the time of the Emperor Diocletian down to the year 1890', while the fourth, revised to November 1898, brought the coverage nearly to the end of the 1890s. Augustus Webb's *Supplement* for the 1900s was a respectful updating: it is pleasing to know, for example, under Mulhall's original entry 'Eggs', what the annual average export of eggs might have become from the Russian Empire, Austria-Hungary, Italy and France in the period 1902–6; the largest exporter was Tsarist Russia, with an average of 27 billion eggs, while the UK, the chief importer, took 2.3 billion.[13] Webb was almost as much a collector of oddities as Mulhall. Mulhall's last *Dictionary* recorded that an offer of £500 was actually *refused* at the Sydenham cat show of 1869 (his single Dictionary entry under 'cats'), that there were at least 50,000 statistical works extant, and that China exported 'a large number of paper-covered umbrellas'.

These are unimportant, no doubt, even if they do serve to indicate the intellectual division between generations. Mulhall was but one of a breed: F. X. von Neumann-Spallart, *Uebersichten der Weltwirtschaft* (Stuttgart, 1878 and subsequent editions to 1895), *Porter, *McCulloch and *Macgregor, Jules Beloch's articles on world demography in the *Zeitschrift für Sozialwissenschaft* in 1899 and 1900, *Cairnes, Albert Scobel's *Geographisches Handbuch* (Bielefeld, 1899), and a whole bevy of French statisticians back to the encyclopedists and *idéologues* of the mid-eighteenth century. But since Mulhall is employed so continually, it may be worth following through his entry for 'world' trade.

Under 'Commerce', Mulhall's *Dictionary* (fourth edition) took 'world trade', imports and exports, back to 1720; besides Europe and Turkey, his coverage included Spanish America, the British colonies, India and £5 million for 'various'; the total for the 'world' in 1720 was £8 million. The last figure arrived at in Mulhall's estimates, for 'world' trade in 1889, was £3,377,000,000. This was then broken down by imports and exports of all nations from 1861 to 1886, the commerce of the principal nations compared with the size of their populations (for 1830, 1870 and 1889), and even the 'non-continuous records of British commerce since the time of Edward III'.

Official returns for Britain's overseas trade were published by the Board of Trade in comprehensible form from 1854, and Mulhall could draw also on what might be thought to be the less convincing evidence of 'Dobbs' on Ireland in the seventeenth century and Leone Levi on 'Italy' for 1850 (i.e. *before* Unification). But 'official returns', said to be the basis of Mulhall's totals, look more vulnerable when the foreign trade of Argentina appeared 'quantified' from 1795 (imports and exports *per capita*) and the same for Uruguay from 1841, at a time when even the United States could supply no convincing export statistics before 1820 and import data were incomplete. US trade statistics remained highly suspect throughout the nineteenth century. Germany's trade statistics meant very little before 1880. It is fanciful to think (with Mulhall) that the foreign trade of 'Turkey' – presumably some unspecified proportion of the Ottoman Empire – could be enumerated from as early as 1854, or that there was really a satisfactory figure for the total trade of the Empire of Persia ('said to reach £7,700,000').[14]

Some genuine figures survive, of which those for railways in most countries are outstanding. But it is less interesting to find, under 'Hunting', that 30 million hares and rabbits were shot in the United Kingdom annually to the value of £2.2 million, or, under 'Insects', that there were 26,800 worms to each acre of land in the United Kingdom. A sympathetic entry in the *Dictionary of National Biography* found Mulhall's *Dictionary* a 'standard book of reference . . . few modern compilations have been more extensively used or abused'; Mulhall had been 'charged with guess-work', but this was unfair, for even if some of his data were far from being as trustworthy as could be desired,

> his deductions are all carefully worked out, and the whole volume [the *Dictionary*] was most carefully printed, owing to the indefatigable zeal of his proof corrector, Marion Mulhall (born Murphy), whom he had married in Buenos Aires in 1878.[15]

Mulhall could hardly have been unaware of the extent of the problems he faced. By 1887 he had already joined the statisticians of rival nations (the United States, Germany and France) in their fashionable search for the comparative wealth of nations. Mulhall's own celebratory volume, *Fifty Years of National Progress, 1837–1887* (London, 1887), was drawn almost entirely from published British figures, although (without sources) he was prepared to compare Britain's price-level with the 'price-level of the world' for 1851–60 and then up to 1881–84.[16]

A decade later, Mulhall's *Industries and Wealth of Nations* (London, 1896) calculated the 'wealth' of nations at 'almost 70 millions sterling'. In reality Mulhall's 'world' survey covered only twenty countries, almost all European. He began his book with an epigraph from Leroy-Beaulieu: 'We must avoid the absurdity of limiting Statistics to ascertained facts, for in many cases this branch of science can reach only approximate results.'[17] But he was irrepressible. In a short 'addendum' to his Appendix, Mulhall reported that 'official documents' had just arrived from Rome to show that the manual energy of Italy was not 2,750 millions of foot-tons daily, as given on page 189, but 2,940, and if water power in Italian factories (1894) reached 250,000 horse power, and this were included, the total energy of Italy would be 13,260 millions of foot-tons daily, say 428 foot-tons per inhabitant.[18] Sources were not supplied.

THE MODERNS: B. R. MITCHELL AND WILLIAM WOODRUFF

The numbers we gather nowadays are (of course) better researched. They are (normally) fully acknowledged. B. R. Mitchell, for example, has assembled a mass of historical statistics. His *Abstract of British Historical Statistics* (Cambridge, 1962), prepared in collaboration with *Phyllis Deane, was aimed simply at the United Kingdom, while his trade statistics (Board of Trade) take account of the changes in Britain's official methodology after 1854. However, the 'balance of payments' calculations are taken, without comment, from *Imlah.[19] Mitchell's *Second Abstract* (Cambridge, 1971) simply updated the figures for British overseas trade from 1938 to 1965, including the 'Balance of Payments'; it made no alterations to the numbers before 1938.[20]

The basis for Mitchell's *European Historical Statistics 1750–1970* (London, 1975) is more open to doubt. The British 'balance of payments' figures remained unaltered. To 1900 they came from *Imlah for 'Visible Balance', 'Invisible Balance' and 'Overall Current Balance'. Thereafter, they are taken, 1900 to 1958, from *Charles Feinstein's *National Income, Expenditure and Output of the United Kingdom, 1855–1965* (Cambridge, 1972). But Feinstein, to 1913, is simply an improved version of Imlah where 'Feinstein treats all visible trade f.o.b., whereas Imlah takes imports c.i.f.', and Feinstein had 'adjusted the trade returns to include diamonds and second hand ships'.[21] So Imlah's weird figures for Britain's 'Balance of Payments' to 1913, published in 1958, turn up again in modified form in Feinstein (1972) and are reproduced uncritically by B.R. Mitchell three years later.

Mitchell's figures outside Britain are again 'official'. He is entirely aware of the problems to be expected from 'official' figures. As government statistics from European countries they are more valuable than most, although material drawn from Portugal's 'official' *Annuario Estatistico* from 1875 and, even more so, from Spain's *Anuario Estadístico* from 1858, might raise some eyebrows. And it is not so absolutely clear to me, whatever it may be to others, that the miscellaneous government material for *foreign* countries published in Britain's *Parliamentary Papers*, on which Mitchell relies without explanation, can be employed without further reference.

The problem of sources remains. When William Woodruff gave us a table on 'Growth of World Trade and Percentage of it held by

Europe, Leading Commercial Countries and the United States', we were told that the source, before 1914, was 'rough estimates based on M. G. Mulhall, *The Dictionary of Statistics* (1899)', while the figures for 1913, although not so precisely identified, seem to have come either from the *League of Nation's *International Statistical Yearbook* or from *The Statesman's Yearbook.*[22] The figures for 'world' population before the First World War in Woodruff's *Impact of Western Man* came from *Carr-Saunders' the **Demographic Yearbooks* of the United Nations and the *Woytinskys. Woodruff's estimates for British investment abroad (amount and distribution) at the outbreak of the First World War, came obviously from *Feis, and show the usual confusion between 'flow' and 'stock'.[23]

THE EARLY DEMOGRAPHERS

'World' population statistics are particularly strange, and stranger still when employed to 'prove', say, the relative decline of per capita income between the Third and First Worlds. Demography is a world of its own into which it is perilous for the non-specialist to wander – a parish in which *Imre Ferenczi and *Walter Willcox are republished in a solemn series, *Demographic Monographs*, edited by economists and sociologists from the Universities of Pennsylvania and Pittsburgh. I do not intend to question demographic professionalism for more recent times; I am simply an unskilled but sceptical historian with some notion of problems in historical quantification for the Third World.

My question, then, must be the source of numbers for 'world' population before the Second World War. How legitimate is it to employ these figures, broken down in whatever combination, for comparison and deduction? The League of Nations, in the late 1920s, lamented the lack of a regular census in many Asiatic and certain other countries, while 'even the census figures of the native population in Africa, South America and other parts of the world are often conjectural in character'. Certainly, for 1926, the 'lack of exact information concerning the movement of population in China necessarily renders the calculations for Asia open to doubt'. But, as always with the League, there is a certain insouciance in its approach to 'world' figures over the *longue durée*. After reporting these and other (most proper) grounds for unease, the League's officials concluded that there was no reason to doubt that an estimated 'world' population at the end of 1926 (very doubtful in itself) of little over 6 per cent greater than it had been in 1913 (hideously doubtful) was, all the same, in the 'right order of magnitude'.[24]

If I may return to the sources, I find that Jules Beloch[25] was the source of Quincy Wright's 'world' population figures up to 1600,[26] and Quincy Wright the source for Bennett's.[27] M. K. Bennett, Director of the Food Research Institute at Stanford, wrote an agreeable little book 'with inexpert readers in mind' in which he showed the slow increase of the population of Europe from 400 years before Christ. This was taken from 'the opinions of the most competent scholars' (otherwise unspecified). After 1650, Bennett's figures came from *Willcox and *Carr-Saunders.[28]

Walter F. Willcox, Professor of Economics and Statistics at Cornell, was the leading 'world' demographer of the inter-war years. His opinions on such questions as the population of China in the 1920s and 1930s were 'taken very seriously into consideration by the League's officers'.[29] The 'long-range view' subscribed to by the United Nations for world population 1650–1900 was based primarily on Willcox.[30]

Willcox was a fanatical collector of numbers. His *Studies in American Demography* (Ithaca, New York, 1940) contained a chapter on the 'Population of the World and its Modern Increase' that illustrated his approach to sources. Willcox reviewed the many attempts that had been made to produce 'world' estimates, most of which he rightly rejected. Yet he himself then came up with a compromise, taken from the 'best contemporary estimates', for the population of the 'world' in the mid-seventeenth century, another (using and revising as many contemporary estimates as he could find) for the population of the 'world' in 1750, a further estimate for 1800, and yet another for 1850. From these Willcox compiled his own Table 19 ('Estimated Population of the World and Its Distribution by Continents, 1650–1935').

Some guesses are better than others, and Willcox's may be better than most. He was certainly prolific. The 'Bibliography of the More Important Writings of the Author', published by the Emeritus Professor at the end of his distinguished career (*Studies in American Demography*), listed well over one hundred items, many of which, admittedly, were but reviews or contributions to encyclopedias. But Willcox, like all others in this backwater of scholarship, was simply guessing, and those who have followed him would do well to acknowledge it. In inexpert hands, Willcox's untestable contentions on the relative growth and decline of the populations of Asia and Europe yield odd results. His view that the figures he had gathered for 1650 and 1750 'probably should be [trusted] until superseded' is questionable, and he concluded, after some embarrassing remarks on racial composition, with a quotation from an earlier authority (1778) in which it was acknowledged that figures were 'only a first step towards the truth', but that the only 'proper way to criticize them is to displace them by more accurate figures'.[31] This cannot be serious.

Willcox, when editor of *Internal Migrations* for the National Bureau of Economic Research, had delegated the calculation of immigration figures to Imre Ferenczi. Ferenczi took some short cuts. He published, among others, a figure of 35,000 for migration from 'Africa' (1846–50), the only basis of which was immigration into Mauritius. He admitted in his text – although this might well be missed by seekers after his tables – that continental migrations in Asia, America, Oceania and Africa could not be compared with European movements. He added (in a footnote) that

> genuine migration statistics, distinguishing overseas from continental migrants and taking account of the more important movements of native labor, were introduced after the [First World] War.[32]

Willcox and Ferenczi had their limitations when it came to the figures for 'world' population after 1650, and they knew it. The problems start when *Bennett quoted *Willcox and *Ferenczi and Bennett then became the source for others. I have mentioned that Bennett took figures from Carr-Saunders. Sir Alexander Carr-Saunders, an impressive source, published his estimates under the auspices of the Royal Institute of International Affairs, another impressive source. He discussed the causes and consequences of the 'immense' expansion since 1650, and indicated the problems which had arisen from world population increase by the mid-1920s. Effectively, Carr-Saunders took his numbers from *Willcox before 1933, and from the *League of Nations thereafter.[33] Then, 'world' population appeared in the appropriate volume of the *Cambridge Economic History of Europe* (1965). By now the estimates had become solid and respectable. But percentage distribution and rate of increase in 1900 were derived, all the same, from Carr-Saunders, who had taken them in turn from *Willcox; the source for 1850 and 1900 was *Willcox; from

1920 the numbers belong to the *United Nations inherited from the *League of Nations.[34]

WORLD COMMERCE AND DEMOGRAPHY: THE WOYTINSKYS

Mr and Mrs Woytinsky's vast excavations into 'world' statistics were rescued and published by the *Twentieth Century Fund. They appeared as *World Population and Production* (New York, 1953) and *World Commerce and Governments: Trends and Outlook* (New York, 1955), two huge volumes of random statistics. Evans Clark, Executive Director of the Fund, admired their efforts, without the help of research contributors or collaborators, after 'years of residence and study in the United States and European countries, with knowledge of several languages and extensive travel in both industrialised and underdeveloped countries' to create

> what amounts to a statistical picture of the collected resources, as well as the economic performance and promise, of the full array of the nations of the world.[35]

This may or may not have become true for the more recent decades: Evans Clark, having taken responsibility for publishing this compendium, was obliged to sell it. But the earlier figures, from which projections are habitually made, are hardly convincing. In their first volume on 'world population', the Woytinskys drew their 1846–1924 figures from *Willcox and *Ferenczi.[36] Their researches (Volume II) included choice specimens from Albert Scobel which in turn derived from 'Jurashek', where 'world' trade in 1820, exports and imports, totalled probably £110/£120 million, rising by 1867–8 to nearly £1 billion for world exports and £1.1 billion for imports.[37] The Woytinskys took Scobel as far as he went (late 1890s); the figures for trade came subsequently from the *League of Nations' *Memorandum on Balance of Payments and Foreign Trade*.[38]

These, supposedly, are the figures for 'world' trade *and* 'world' population into the 1930s, from which many 'per capita' sums are derived. They are widely cited, and were published under distinguished patronage.

Notes

1. F. W. Hirst (ed.), *G. R. Porter's Progress of the Nation* (new, updated and revised edn, London, 1912) p. v.
2. G. R. Porter, *The Progress of the Nation* (London, 1851 edn,).
3. Hirst, *Porter's Progress of the Nation*, p. vii.
4. John Macgregor, *The Resources and Statistics of Nations* (London, 1834) p. 6.
5. *Ibid.*, pp. 2, 12–13.
6. *Ibid.*, p. 464.
7. Macgregor, *Commercial Statistics*, Vol. II (London, 1844) p. 7.
8. Preface to Michael G. Mulhall, *Mulhall's Dictionary of Statistics* (London, 1884).
9. Mulhall, *The Progress ofthe World* (1880) pp. 17 and 16.
10. *Ibid.*, p. 39.
11. Mulhall, *Balance Sheet of the World for the Ten Years 1870–1880* (London, 1881) p. 138.
12. Cited in the prelims of the second edition (1886).
13. Augustus Webb, *New Dictionary of Statistics* (London, 1911) p. 231.
14. Mulhall, *Dictionary of Statistics* (fourth edn, London, 1899) pp. 128–55.
15. T.S. in the *Dictionary of National Biography*, Vol. XXII Supplement.
16. Mulhall, *Fifty Years of National Progress 1837–1887* (London, 1887) p. 28.
17. Mulhall, *Industries and Wealth of Nations* (London, 1896) p. vii.
18. *Ibid.*, p. 433.
19. B. R. Mitchell, *Abstract of British Historical Statistics* (Cambridge, 1962) pp. 333–4.
20. Mitchell and H. G. Jones, *Second Abstract of British Historical Statistics* (Cambridge, 1971). Feinstein's faith in Imlah still survives: *Studies in Capital Formation in the United Kingdom, 1750–1920* (Oxford, 1988) p. 396
21. Mitchell, *European Historical Statistics 1750–1970* (London, 1975) pp. 817–27.
22. William Woodruff, *Impact of Western Man: A Study of Europe's Role in the World Economy 1750–1960* (London, 1966) Table VII/12 (p. 313), p. 334 (for world trade), p. 103 (world population).
23. *Ibid.*, Tables IV/1 and IV/3 on pp. 150, 154 and 155.
24. Economic and Financial Section, League of Nations, *Memorandum on Production and Trade 1913 and 1923/6* (Geneva, 1928) p. 14.
25. Beloch's articles, referred to in the main text above, and in the *Zeitschrift für Sozialwissenschaft* (1899 and 1900).
26. Quincy Wright was Professor of International Law at the University of Chicago, and the author of many books. The population figures, prior to 1600, are in Table III, Appendix V, of his *A Study of War*, Vol. I (Chicago, 1942) p. 467.
27. M. K. Bennett, *The World's Food: A Study of the Interrelations of World Populations, Natural Diets and Food Potentials* (New York, 1954).
28. *Ibid.*, pp. 5–9.

29. Economic Intelligence Service, League of Nations, *World Economic Survey 1931–2* (Geneva, 1932) p. 12, fn. 2.
30. Department of Social Affairs, Population Division, United Nations, *Population Bulletin No. 1* (New York, December 1951) p. 2.
31. Walter F. Willcox, *Studies in American Demography* (Ithaca, New York, 1940) p. 51.
32. Imre Ferenczi in Walter F. Willcox (ed.), *International Migrations*, Vol. I, *Statistics* (New York, 1929) p. 223 and fn. 1.
33. A. M. Carr-Saunders, *World Population: Past Growth and Present Trends* (Oxford, 1936) pp. xii–xiii, 30.
34. D. V. Glass and E. Grebenik, 'World Population, 1800–1950', in H. J. H. Habakkuk and M. Postan (eds), *Cambridge Economic History of Europe*, Vol. VI, 'The Industrial Revolutions and After' (Cambridge, 1965) pp. 57–8.
35. Foreword to W. S. and E. S. Woytinsky, *World Population and Production: Trends and Outlook* (New York, 1953) p. v.
36. Woytinsky, *World Population and Production*, p. 77.
37. Albert Scobel, *Geographisches Handbuch zu Andrees Allgemeiner Handatlas* (Bielefeld, 1899) p. 680.
38. Woytinsky, *World Commerce and Governments: Trends and Outlook* (New York, 1955) p. 39.

2 Governments and International Institutions

Profound respect is paid to the published figures of the great international institutions; they acquire the stamp of authenticity by provenance alone: the League of Nations, the Royal Institute of International Affairs, the Carnegie Endowment for International Peace, the United Nations, the Economic Commission for Latin America, the Twentieth Century Fund, the Geneva Agreement on Tariffs and Trade. . . .

I have mentioned already the publications of the *Carnegie Endowment – the patronage bestowed on the aged *Woytinskys, procurers of unlikely statistics – and I wonder whether the search for 'relevant' material overcame prudence and scholarship. Elsewhere I have annotated the progress through Britain's Chancellor of the Exchequer, the Board of Trade, the Royal Institute of International Affairs, the League of Nations and the United Nations, of an unreliable number for the stock of Britain's investment overseas on the eve of the First World War, shakily constructed from the estimates of the Chancellor's adviser, Sir George Paish.[1] The travels of that number, through politics (national and international), scholarship and the text-books, have consolidated a pre-First World War estimate (intended for an altogether different purpose) to the point where it has become the conventional wisdom of the 1980s.

THE STATISTICS OF FOREIGN COUNTRIES BEFORE 1914: BRITAIN'S BOARD OF TRADE

'Official' papers hold special charms, perhaps particularly for those reared within a modern generation in which government records are more consistent and reliable. *John R. Hanson attaches great importance to such 'foreign' data as the Board of Trade was able to find and publish over the nineteenth century; other countries, including the United States, made occasional attempts to do the same. Yet their value is rather less than one might be led to suppose.

The British government published its own trade figures, in one form or another, from the 1830s. Some 'Trade Accounts of Foreign

Countries' were added in the 1860s, but they were limited to those of Belgium, Holland, France, Switzerland and the United States. Returns of total imports and exports were supplied at five-yearly intervals from 1854 to 1889, but these were again limited, this time to eleven Western European countries and the United States. No source was given, but the material was clearly 'official', and it was supplied only 'so far as the information can be given'.[2] The returns were brought up to 1897 by the Board of Trade[3] and then to 1904,[4] yet they were for the identical range of countries and carried the identical warning (i.e. 'so far as the information can be given'). It was a slender basis on which to calculate 'world' trade.

On investigation the same is true of the broader range of international statistics apparently on offer in the British government's *Memorandum on the Comparative Statistics of Population, Industry, and Commerce in the United Kingdom and some Leading Foreign Countries*, published in 1897.[5] The Board of Trade had been asked to examine Britain's home and foreign trade in recent years, and to compare it with similar statistics of leading countries such as France and Germany. The published comparison was therefore confined to France, Germany and the United States, including, beyond trade, some figures for population, urban distribution and 'one or two leading industries'. The result fell far short of 'world' trade, population and industry. The return was supplemented and brought up to date by the Commercial Department of the Board of Trade in May 1902, but it was again limited to Britain's 'principal industrial and trading competitors' (France, Germany and the United States).

More valuable in the present context was a compilation published by the Board of Trade in 1930: *Statistical Tables relating to British and Foreign Trade and Industry (1924–30)*. It included a table, under 'foreign trade', that seemed to show 'World Trade in 1913, 1924 and 1927–29' based on 'the official returns of trade from 175 countries or trading areas'. Its coverage was rather more extensive than a similar exercise undertaken by the *League of Nations. But as the Board explained, the figures for 1913 were not strictly comparable with those for the post-war era because of boundary changes and the creation of new states, 'quite apart from the changes in the level of values',[6] so that the 'official' sources quoted for the 'rest of Europe', 'Africa', the 'rest of Asia', and the 'rest of North and South America' (once the main countries were included) were not as useful as they might have been.

The Board's 'official' figures for 1913 were thus as vulnerable, certainly for the 'Third World', as those of the League of Nations. For the 1920s, indeed, they must be used with care. From 1924–5 to 1928–9 Britain's Board of Trade employed the numbers printed in the *League's *Memorandum on International Trade and Balances of Payments* for the import and export trades of the 'world' by continental areas and groups.[7] The League's figures, in turn, were based on the official returns of sixty-four countries, on the questionable assumption that these countries supplied 95.7 per cent of the 'world's' imports and exports.[8] The assumption was convenient for the international bureaucracy, but no references are given. Bearing in mind the difficulty of measuring trade between Third World countries, particularly over land frontiers, they are quite unprovable.

In the great range of statistics published by the British government, the most often reported are the *Statistical Tables relating to Foreign Countries*. From 1844 the Board of Trade, under the direction of *G. R. Porter, began collecting and publishing foreign statistical returns as a supplement to its *Annual Volume of Tables relating to the Revenue, Population, Commerce etc. of the United Kingdom*.[9] These were a haphazard group of tables gathered when and where possible and sent home by British consulates and diplomatic missions abroad; the only reference to Mexico, for example, in the first (1844) issue, was a 'Statement of the Coinage in Gold and Silver of the Mints of the Mexican Republic, in the Years 1839 and 1840'. The figures, reliable or not, were random, unexplained and unascribed.

From the mid-1850s, volumes of foreign statistics appeared separately and somewhat spasmodically under the better-known title *Statistical Tables relating to Foreign Countries*. These were described, once more, as having been 'compiled, for the most part, from the official returns of the respective countries'. The Statistical Department of the Board of Trade, now under the direction of A. W. Fonblanque, collected the best figures it could find. The first volume of the new, independent series, for 1854–5, gave a selection of figures for Russia, Sweden, Norway and Denmark, in great quantity but without explanation or provenance. The second volume provided a similar selection for the Zollverein states of Germany.[10]

The British series undoubtedly brought together and published a large range of data, in a single language and in accessible form. The quality of the statistics naturally improved; over time they became more comprehensive and better organised. A. E. Bateman, of the Statistical Department of the Board of Trade, compiled a *Statistical Abstract for the Principal and Other Foreign Countries from 1888 to*

1897–8 ('as far as the Particulars can be stated') which supplied a mass of information, some of value for comparison, even for countries beyond Europe and the United States such as Mexico, Chile, Uruguay, Argentina, China and Japan. It related to imports and exports, agriculture and livestock, railways (length, cost of construction, traffic, etc.), telegraphs, post, emigration/immigration, finance (for Europe and the United States), and miscellaneous figures for coinage, the beet sugar industry, mining production (for Europe and the United States), fisheries (Norway, Holland and France), spirit production in France. . . .[11] The sources were given as 'official', but not otherwise identified.

The *Statistical Abstract*, except occasionally and tangentially, is not of great value for the history of the Third World. More can be expected from the first and subsequent issues of the *Statistical Abstract for the British Empire* (from 1905), giving figures from 1889. Since the British Empire at the time took in so much of what was to become the Third World, the data are of interest over a wide field – trade, shipping and production (mineral, agricultural and pastoral).

British imperial returns, like any other statistics, must be treated with care: 'trade' seldom took account of re-exports of imported goods, the entrepôt ports of Hong Kong, Malta and Gibraltar were excluded, and the trade of the British Protectorates was likewise omitted. Population statistics that gave the Native States of British India 54.8 million in 1881, compared with 199 million in British India, were based on a census of 1881 that could hardly have been carried out in detail. Is it possible that the population of Sierra Leone in 1881 was 31,201 males and 29,345 females, or that of Lagos 37,665 males and 37,605 females? Or are we attaching accuracy and importance to the efforts of tired and over-heated colonial officials summoned by the Imperial Government to make a nonsensical return? From the 1881 census, the whole population of the Empire, including the United Kingdom, was estimated at 303.2 million inhabitants; by 1901 this number had risen to 360.6 million. Or had it? These were figures that were intended, as the Board explained, to meet the 'growing demand for statistical information' about the British Empire and its relations within itself and with foreign countries.[12] It was a part of the fair trade/free trade debate. Might not its objectivity, in 1905, be in doubt?

By 1914 Britain's *Statistical Abstract for the Principal and Other Foreign Countries* had reached its thirty-ninth edition. Many countries were now included, but references – other than the simple distinction between 'official' and 'unofficial' – were still neither given nor more generally explained. The *Statistical Abstract* (1914) quoted Venezuela's population census of 1891 and Peru's of 1876. Many figures for trade, shipping, production and consumption were given for as many parts of the world, but again without precise citation or warning.[13] The statistics supplied for Britain itself were as well-administered in 1914 as any, but there are enormous difficulties if they are taken for more than they claimed to be. Understandably, there continued to be a shortage of real data for the world outside the British Empire. Even within the Empire, the minute bureaucracy of the day ensured that much of the information it returned was what we might now call 'creative accounting'. The modern scholar recoils, quite rightly, at the absence of references, the inability to check and double-check. The volume of statistical material published for Britain's Parliament is overwhelmingly impressive, the quality is less certain, and little help is given towards evaluation.

THE LEAGUE OF NATIONS

The League's statistics are taken normally from the composite volume *Industrialization and Foreign Trade*, prepared for the League by *Folke Hilgerdt and published in Geneva in 1945. The League pointed to the fragility of the figures up to 1913, but it then proceeded, without reference other than to itself, to publish figures for 'world trade' back to 1871. On examination, these 'world' statistics were notably incomplete, and most began much later – Japan, for example, in 1891–5, and British Dominions from 1901; furthermore, there were no pre-First World War figures for Africa, Latin America, British colonies or other colonial empires.[14]

It is never easy to follow the League's method: one publication referred to another, which then referred to a third. But ultimately we arrive at the 'explanatory note' to the first volume, 'Trade Statistics of Forty-two Countries', of the League's *Memorandum on International Trade and Balances of Payments, 1910–1923* (Geneva, 1924). This 'note', and a similar note for the third publication 1912–26 (Geneva, 1928), are particularly helpful in identifying the complexities of international trade classification. The explanation is not straightforward. Siam before 1914, as the first 'explanatory note' revealed, had shipped more than 10 per cent of its exports to Egypt 'for orders', while Argentina's exports 'for orders' were usually 25 per cent or more; the final destination was undisclosed. This was the case for *any* country exporting primary produce to distant markets, so that the trade statistics more affected than most were likely to be those of the United Kingdom, France, Belgium, the Netherlands and Germany – the principal customers of the Third World. Indeed, the burden of what the League says in its explanatory notes is that even the 'official' Customs returns on which it exclusively relied, for the 42 countries of the 1924 Memorandum, the 57 for 1925 and the 64 for the 1928 Memorandum (from which much of the Third World was in fact excluded), were seldom satisfactory before 1914.

This was the case, and it was fully and honestly explained. Yet it is on this kind of number that the League itself then calculated a fall in Europe's share of 'world' trade from 58.4 per cent in 1913 to 48.1 per cent in 1926, and a subsequent rise to 50.4 per cent in 1927, while the shares of 'Asia' and North America decreased – 'Asia' rising from 12.1 per cent in 1913 to 16.6 per cent in 1926, and then falling to 15.4 per cent of 'world' trade in 1927.

Obviously, for any kind of comparison or deduction the League's numbers for 1913 are extraordinarily fragile. They could not apply to the new, post-war nations of Europe – Albania, Estonia, Latvia, Lithuania, Poland, Czechoslovakia and the Irish Free State – and these were not inconsiderable; the League itself reported a calculation to the effect that the 1913 population of those European territories detached from their previous allegiances after the 1918–19 settlements 'amounted to nearly 73 millions'.[15] Furthermore, the coverage of Third World countries before 1914 is erratic and very incomplete, under headings like the 'Dutch East Indies', 'British Africa' (which meant, in practice, only the Union of South Africa and Nigeria), and 'British Malaya'. A larger share, unspecified, is accounted for under the unhelpful heading of 'autres pays'.

It should be said that the League's *Memoranda* (on international trade and balance of payments) are by no means unsophisticated or naïve. The warnings in the 1924 and 1928 issues are admirable, and fully maintain the most particular recommendation of the British Association's statisticians of *1904, i.e. that, for the sake of the public who used official publications, a reasoned statement on the accuracy and exact meaning of the returns should always be inserted: 'As it is, it is a matter of the greatest difficulty for even the educated public to attach the right meaning to offical returns.'[16]

The same caution, quite naturally, was displayed by the editors of the League's *International Statistical Yearbooks*. A. Loveday, editor of the first volumes, explained both in 1926 and 1927 that although in the great majority of cases he was using 'official' statistics, it was not always possible to supply good figures. He had supplemented these by the best 'unofficial' sources he could find, but users of the *Yearbooks* were warned that they 'should not attribute to any unofficial compilations any authority greater than that of the source from which they are obtained'.[17]

The League, unfortunately, did not feel the need to observe its own warning. I have explained how one League publication echoed another, during which process the real source was lost and the importance of the 'findings' exaggerated. The League's *Memoranda on Production and Trade 1913 and 1923/6* (published in 1926 and 1928), with subsequent issues into the 1930s, took their figures from the League's own **Memorandum on International Trade and Balances of Payments 1912–1926*, 'in which will be found the detailed statistics of the international trade of the world'. It was unnecessary, the officials argued, yet again to discuss in detail the data upon which their 'world' trade estimates were based, or the principles applied. They were confident that the quantum of world trade (imports and exports together), taken at 100 for 1913, was 154.5 in 1925 and 145 in 1926, from which they deduced the 'failure of world trade as a whole to keep pace with the growth in production'.[18]

So it was from these, as a percentage of the appropriate numbers in 1913, that we are given the population (for 1926) of Europe, the Americas, the Caribbean, Africa, Asia and Oceania, the production of raw materials and foodstuffs, and the quantum of trade, for 1924, 1925 and 1926. Twelve 'conclusions' were then drawn for the change since 1913, including an opinion that 'progress in the rest of the world in recent years has been much more rapid than in Europe', and that 'South American trade is only 4 per cent greater than in 1913'.[19]

This may seem improbable. The League explained how its figures were based on statistics that were sometimes defective and of doubtful comparability; they were 'seldom so comprehensive or so exact as to render it possible to draw conclusions of mathematical accuracy or incontrovertible finality from any single series'. Importance should be attached to trends rather than to absolute magnitudes. But it is at this point that officials refer to other officials (or often the same officials under a different hat). Readers are told to look for the 'important qualifications' in the **Memoranda on International Trade* and to such parallel publications as the *Memoranda on*

Currency and Central Banks.[20] The force of such warnings, by the time they are traced (if at all) through the complicated and ill-referenced publications of the international civil service, are often lost. Few readers have penetrated beyond the 'Summary of Results of Analysis'.

The story is not at an end. The League's *International Statistical Yearbook* for 1926 took its data for international imports and exports in 1913 from its own first *Memorandum on International Trade and Balances of Payments*, and so did the eminently respectable New Zealander, Professor J. B. Condliffe, in his volume *World Economic Survey 1931–2*, edited and published for the League (Geneva, 1932). Condliffe used the *Memorandum*'s comparison of 'world' production in 1913 with 1925, and the associated figures, to construct 'Indices of Production and Trade, 1925' (1913 = 100). The resulting table was 'sufficient to show that, by 1925, Europe had barely recovered its pre-War level of production'. From this precarious base, Condliffe proceeded to argue that over the next five years (1925 to the third quarter of 1929) the quantum of world trade had increased by 19 per cent,[21] which may or may not have been approximately true, but which would be determined by the accuracy of the (questionable) index for 1913.

J. B. Condliffe's *The Commerce of Nations* (London, 1951), which originated in his Henry E. Howland Memorial Lectures at Yale in January 1939, employed *Feis for 'long term international investment in 1914' (British, German and French). Condliffe's figures for 'world consumption of minerals' and 'world power' since 1860 came from the League of Nations. The League of Nations was his source for 'world' trade, 'world' population and percentage shares in 'world' manufacturing production in 1938.[22] For 1946 he brought his figures for 'world' population up to date from the Office of Intelligence Research, US Department of State, and for 'world' trade from the International Monetary Fund.[23] *The Commerce of Nations* is widely based and well presented, but it belongs to the school of international civil servants – indeed, *Folke Hilgerdt is among those acknowledged in the Foreword – for whom the source of a figure, if published under sufficiently impressive authority, remained undiscussed.

THE UNITED NATIONS

It is a mistake to believe that the pre-1940 data employed by the United Nations are an improvement. Naturally the United Nations was responsible for the figures after 1945, but for its earlier data it returned to the League. There is even some physical overlap, since the Economic Commission for Europe (of the United Nations) was actually housed in the League's headquarters at Geneva, and it was the Economic Commission that underwrote Ingvar Svennilson's *Growth and Stagnation in the European Economy* (Geneva, 1954). Svennilson took his 'world' figures up to 1936–1938, for 'world and European exports, 1876–1950' (Table A.58), from the League of Nations' last major publication: *Folke Hilgerdt's *Industrialization and Foreign Trade*. These, in turn, were compiled from the League's inter-war reviews of foreign trade and the **Memoranda on International Trade and Balances of Payments* – that is, the same tables for 'world' trade in manufactured articles and 'world' trade in primary products from 1876. Svennilson's indices for the United Nations back to 1913 were in fact calculated from the League's figures. It was all a little in-bred, even more so when one realises that *Imre Ferenczi, the demographer responsible for *International Migrations*, Vol. I Statistics (New York, 1929) in *Walter Willcox's series for the National Bureau of Economic Research, was attached to the International Labour Office at Geneva, from which he compiled the statistics and wrote the Introduction and Notes. The figures presented by the International Labour Office, the League of Nations and the United Nations, were derived from the same sources.

Nonetheless, those who have used them have often believed that they *reinforced* each other. The very name United Nations, quite apart from the grandeur of the League and the ILO, carries a certain cachet, so that the figures published under its imprint have a habit of leaking into the conventional wisdom. Officials have always welcomed a convenient summary under a distinguished name – it can fill a gap where even the international agencies fear to tread. The first issue of the United Nations' *Population Bulletin*, December 1951, began with a 'long-range view' based on *Professor Walter Willcox for 1650–1900 and on the 1900 estimate for 'Africa' delivered by *Sir Alexander Carr-Saunders. The approach seems almost scholarly by comparison with the United Nations' calculation that if the first couple of *homo sapiens* (Adam and Eve) gave birth in 25,000 BC, an annual rate of increase of 0.7 per thousand would generate a world population of 350 million by the birth of Christ, so that the average rate of population growth from 1650 to 1950 was 'at least eight times as large as that before the Christian era'.[24]

Of course, this was the 'long-range view' which officials have always felt obliged to furnish before proceeding to a series beginning realistically only from the 1920s: they themselves (we must hope) were unlikely to have taken it seriously. The problem is that these numbers began to appear as if endorsed by the United Nations. Method has much improved since then (1951), but it is interesting that, twenty years later, in *The Determinants and Consequences of Population Trends*, the United Nations was still prepared to estimate 'world population' at 5–10 million in 7000/6000 BC, while the figures from 1750, including Africa, Asia and Latin America, came yet again from *Willcox and *Carr-Saunders. The population of the world is now said to be approaching 5 billion, from which all kinds of alarmist deductions may be drawn (*The Times*, 6 July 1987). This naturally begins with *Willcox's 'best contemporary estimate', some 500 million in 1650!

The absurdities of 'world' historical demography are obvious, and they are mentioned in my previous chapter. They alarm only when an international agency seems to legitimise and convey authority. 'World' trade, 'balances of payments', 'terms of trade' are similarly authenticated. From 1956 the United Nations published, as *International Trade Statistics*, an annual continuation of the League's *Memoranda*. The United Nations absorbed what it could from the League.[25] The disease spread, quite naturally, to the Agencies. ECLA (CEPAL) – the Economic Commission for Latin America – took pride in publishing Argentine figures back to 1900. Since ECLA was headed by the well-known Argentine economist, Raúl Prebisch, and could draw on the figures of Alberto Martínez from well before the First World War, Argentine figures back to 1900 were possible, although sources were not supplied and the references were published separately only in mimeographed form (a nasty trick to play on the serious scholar). All the same, numbers for the accumulation of capital per capita, foreign capital as a percentage of total fixed capital, movements of capital and external payments, and distribution of capital between occupations, go beyond what might be expected from Argentina's statistical office or from Martínez's genuinely excellent researches.[26] The exercise became even less convincing when CEPAL calculated GDP for Argentina from 1899, and from 1929 for Brazil, Chile and Colombia. It becomes positively terrifying when CEPAL suggests, from its patchy data, 'posibles soluciones'.[27]

Notes

1. D. C. M. Platt, *Britain's Investment Overseas on the Eve of First World War: The Use and Abuse of Numbers* (London, 1986) pp. 7–8.
2. 'Return of Total Imports and Exports for Each Year 1854, 1859, 1864, 1869, 1874, 1879, 1884 and 1889 of 12 Countries', *British Parliamentary Papers*, 1890–1891, LXXVII, pp. 348–9.
3. *Parliamentary Papers*, 1898, LXXXIV, pp. 360–1.
4. *Ibid.*, 1906, CXIV, pp. 652–3.
5. *Ibid.*, 1897, LXXXIII, pp. 707–58.
6. 'Tables Relating to the External Trade of the United Kingdom, the Dominions and India with Foreign Countries, Distinguishing Principal Classes of Goods', *Parliamentary Papers*, 1930–31, XXXI, pp. 184–5.
7. *Ibid.*, pp. 186–93.
8. League of Nations, Economic and Financial Section, *Memorandum on Production and Trade 1913 and 1923–6* (Geneva, 1928) p. 13.
9. Supplement to Part XII, *Parliamentary Papers*, 1844, XLVI, pp. 529ff.
10. The first separate publication was in *Parliamentary Papers*, 1854/5, LII, pp. 533ff.
11. 'Statistical Abstract for the Principal and Other Foreign Countries in Each Year from 1888 to 1897–98', *Parliamentary Papers*, 1900, XCVIII, pp. 275ff.
12. 'Statistical Abstract of the British Empire in each year from 1889 to 1903', *Parliamentary Papers*, 1905, XCIV, pp. 319ff.
13. 'Statistical Abstract for the Principal and Other Foreign Countries in each year from 1901 to 1912', *Parliamentary Papers*, 1914, XCVII, pp. 305ff.
14. League of Nations, Economic, Financial and Transit Department, *Industrialization and Foreign Trade* (Geneva, 1945), Tables X-XIII, pp. 166–7. The author was *Folke Hilgerdt.
15. League of Nations, Economic and Financial Section, *Memorandum on Production and Trade, 1913 and 1923–6* (Geneva, 1928) p. 13.
16. British Association for the Advancement of Science, Report of the Committee on the Accuracy and Comparability of British and Foreign Statistics of International Trade, in the *Annual Report* (London, 1904) p. 317.
17. League of Nations, Economic and Financial Section, *International Statistical Year-Books for 1926 and 1927* (Geneva, 1927 and 1928) p. 7.
18. League of Nations, Economic and Financial Section, *Memorandum on Production and Trade 1913 and 1923/6* (Geneva, 1927) pp. 46–7.

19. *Ibid.*, pp. 8–10.
20. *Ibid.*, pp. 46–7.
21. For the League of Nations, J. B. Condliffe (ed.), *World Economic Survey, 1931–2* (Geneva, 1932) pp. 22–4.
22. Condliffe, *The Commerce of Nations* (London, 1951) pp. 327, 299 and 443, 575.
23. *Ibid.*, pp. 683, 707.
24. United Nations, Department of Social Affairs: Population Division, *Population Bulletin*, No. 1 (New York, December 1951) p. 2.
25. United Nations, Economic Commission for Europe, *Growth and Stagnation in the European Economy* (Geneva, 1954) Table A. 58. The author was Ingvar Svennilson.
26. Comisión Económica para América Latina (CEPAL, i.e. ECLA), *El Desarrollo Económico de la Argentina*, Vol. I, 'problemas y perspectivas del crecimiento argentino' (Mexico, 1959) *passim*.
27. *Ibid.*, p. xii.

Part II
The Reapers

3 The Great Generation

By the 1920s the process of data accumulation was well advanced; the ample results were employed by a new generation. Attention now turned to the 'theory' of international trade.

F. W. TAUSSIG AND JACOB VINER

Jacob Viner, the Canadian economist, was Professor of Economics first at Chicago and then at Princeton. His book, *Studies in the Theory of International Trade* (Chicago, 1937), is a scholarly work dedicated to his 'teacher and friend', F. W. Taussig; it analysed the history of foreign trade theory from figures (for before 1914) drawn simply from Viner's previous work, *Canada's Balance of International Indebtedness, 1900–1913* (Cambridge, Mass., 1924).

Taussig himself, Professor of Economics at Harvard in the 1920s, was as cautious as anyone who works professionally with figures; the difficulty, with him and others, was that the caution expressed in the preface was not always reproduced in the main text. For Taussig the problem, as he described it in *International Trade* (1927), was 'the lack of statistical material put together in such a way as to throw light on the validity of the theoretic conclusions'.[1] Yet even for Taussig the temptation proved too great. In his chapter on 'Great Britain: The Terms of Trade, 1880–1914', his figures (very slightly modified) for the excess of Britain's imports over exports, British income from abroad, shipping earnings and the export of capital, came from *C. K. Hobson.[2]

THE 'STOCKHOLM GROUP' AND GUNNAR MYRDAL

Taussig and Viner are the great names of international trade theory for the inter-war decades. But very much a part of the same body was the 'Stockholm Group': Ohlin, Wicksell, Bagge, Brisman, Cassel, Hecksher and Myrdal.

Bertil Gotthard Ohlin of the Stockholm School of Economics (Nobel 1977) was essentially a theorist, and the work for which he is best known, *Interregional and International Trade* (published first by Harvard in 1933 and republished as recently as 1967), is short on facts and figures. Subsequently, Ohlin prepared his *International Economic Reconstruction: An Economists' and Businessmen's Survey of the Main Problems of the Day* (1936), at the instance of a joint committee of the Carnegie Endowment for International Peace and the International Chamber of Commerce in Paris. He was submitting a standard report for which no precise references were given. But it is clear that the sources for *Interregional and International Trade* (1933), re-employed in *International Economic Reconstruction* (1936), were *Feis and *Hobson for British capital exports, and *Taussig for international trade.

Ohlin acknowledged *Gunnar Myrdal, the grand old man of the economics of underdeveloped nations and a joint winner of the Nobel prize for economics (1974), as one of the 'Stockholm' influences on his own 'general theoretical background'.[3] It was the growing indignation of Myrdal at the plight of the underdeveloped world that characterised the Stockholm approach. Myrdal's 'broad vista', the disintegration of the world after the Second World War as compared with 1913, expressed so strongly in his books *International Economy; Problems and Prospects* (1956) and *Economic Theory and Underdeveloped Regions* (1957), was an instinctive piece of personal agonising for which precise data must have seemed intrusive. If Myrdal gave sources at all, they were deeply conventional. International capital movements before 1914 were taken from *The Problem of International Investment*, a doubtful authority published in 1937, on the basis of Sir George Paish's calculations (1913), by the *Royal Institute of International Affairs.[4] Myrdal's 'list of literature' contained all the familiar names: *Folke Hilgerdt, *Simon Kuznets, the *League of Nations, *W. Arthur Lewis, himself (eight works), *Ragnar Nurkse, *Ingvar Svennilson, *Jacob Viner and, above all, the *United Nations. Myrdal's *Asian Drama: An Inquiry into the Poverty of Nations* – a gigantic multi-volume work published in 1968 with the assistance of the *Twentieth Century Fund – drew its figures for 'world' population in 1800, 1850 and 1900 from the *United Nations.[5]

Myrdal means much to many people, and it is clear that, more often than not, his instinct was sound. But anything more precise, from such shaky data, is surely not to be expected. He exemplifies a tradition maintained in the Wicksell Lectures, a distinguished series named after Knut Wicksell, always a leader of the 'Stockholm Group'. The first were given in 1959 by *Ragnar Nurkse, Professor of Economics at Columbia; a decade later the lecturer was *W. Arthur Lewis, then Professor of Economics and International Affairs at Princeton.

RAGNAR NURKSE

In his Wicksell lectures Nurkse took his ideas on changes in the volume of world trade, 1850–1880 and 1880–1913, from an index constructed by *Bertil Ohlin, *International Economic Reconstruction*, which in turn was not 'out of line with' the volume indices for British trade of *A. H. Imlah. Nurkse proceeded to use what he accepted as the 'somewhat incomplete trade matrix' of *W. A. Lewis. Then *Ohlin, *Imlah and *Lewis supplied him with the base for his broad conclusion that

> the intra-trade of Europe and the United States represented as much as 64 per cent of the (incomplete) total of world exports in 1877. Intra-trade in Asia, Africa and South America is not known but was probably small and would not have made much difference to the percentage share of the advanced area's intra-trade.[6]

Nurkse's hypothesis was *foreign* trade as the engine of growth. It may or may not be right (it is furiously disputed). But the indices for 1850 and 1913 were Ohlin's, and *Ohlin gave no source. Similarly, when Nurkse argued the principal rôle taken by the agricultural nations in world trade he was relying on the evidence of *Folke Hilgerdt's publication for the League of Nations, *Industrialization and Foreign Trade* (Geneva, 1945), where Hilgerdt's data on agricultural countries were particularly weak.

W. A. LEWIS

Lewis made more of a speciality of world trade than Nurkse; his Wicksell lectures for 1969 followed the theme of 'tropical trade' from 1883 to 1965. The numbers were based, for 1913, on the *League of Nations; for 1900 he made use of the US Government's *Statistical Abstract for Foreign Countries;* he obtained most of the missing data from the published British and American consular reports, and filled in the 'few' gaps with interpolations. Lewis's weights for prices, and his figures for the volume of world trade in 1913, came from *P. Lamartine Yates, and he linked 1913 to 1925 'on the basis of *A. Maizels, *Industrial Growth and World Trade* (Cambridge, 1963)'. His 'world trade' numbers for 1883 and 1889 'involve some guessing', and the impression must be that Lewis's basis for describing the period 1913 to 1950 as a 'terrible interruption of incipient development' was decidedly weak.[7]

But the Wicksell Lectures were but a single episode. The Nobel Prize followed in 1979. Lewis's reputation in 'world' numbers began with an article, 'World Production, Prices and Trade, 1870–1960' published in the *Manchester School* (1952), in which he acknowledged his debt to the League of Nations for the figures of world trade 1876–1938 as published in *Hilgerdt's *Industrialization and Foreign Trade*.[8]

Lewis's Manchester contemporary, H. Tyszynski, used the same data: *League of Nations to 1938 and the *United Nations thereafter. Tyszynski's 'World Trade in Manufactured Commodities, 1899–1950' employed the eleven countries, 1901–1938, identified by the League in *Industrialization and Foreign Trade*. He then developed a series of tables from the same source, by category and by country, in which 'world' trade was represented by those eleven countries in 'representative years', 1899, 1913, 1929, 1937 and 1950, and where the percentages of each country or commodity in 'world' trade could be calculated to show changes in the structure of trade. From this Tyszynski was able to conclude, resoundingly, that

> between 1899 and 1937 the main reason for the fall of Britain's share in world trade in manufactures was her failure to compete in markets for iron and steel and the engineering products including vehicles.[9]

Much has been published since then, including the Wicksell lectures themselves. But Sir Arthur's work has lasted longer than Tyszynski's, and he is probably best known for his *Growth and Fluctuations 1870–1913* (London, 1978). Table 7.4 for world exports per head, 1913, and annual percentage growth rate of the total for 1883–1913, provide figures for which some basis exists – 'temperate settlements', 'North-West Europe' and the USA, India and Japan. Unfortunately, these figures were quoted alongside the far less convincing columns for 'Other Latin America', 'North Africa', 'S.E. Europe', 'Other Asia', 'Africa (Black)', and China. The data for total trade in 1913 came from *Folke Hilgerdt and the League of Nations, the 1893 figures for tropical countries were guesses from Sir Arthur's own Wicksell Lectures, the weights and the breakdown of trade between manufactures and primary products were from *Lamartine Yates, and the value index was from Lewis's 'World Production' of 1952.

Lewis's *Growth and Fluctuations* was a mammoth effort to deal sensibly with intractable sources. It is indicative that Sir Arthur, when calculating Britain's GDP for 1907, deducted £144 million for interest and dividends from abroad. He took this figure from *Imlah's *Economic Elements in the Pax Britannica*; Imlah took *his* figure, only slightly improved, from Sir George Paish's calculation of income from public and private securities (derived from income tax returns and in part from 'imaginative research').[10] It is perfectly obvious that Lewis accepted Imlah (*Economic Elements*, p. 75) without referring back to its origin (as explained in *Economic Elements*, p. 63).

The pursuit of references can become an obsession, and I am well aware of it. But here we go again. The source of Table 1.1 ('index number of value of exports, 1913') in the introductory chapter to Sir Arthur's edited volume, *Tropical Development 1880–1913: Studies in Economic Progress* (London, 1970), was given as Table 2.1. Table 2.1, as it then appears, was in a paper supplied by one of Lewis's contributors, Charles C. Stover. Stover gave his source as Lewis's Wicksell Lectures; so Lewis, via Stover, cited Lewis . . . But the standard of *Tropical Development* was more than usually low. It was prepared by the members of Lewis's graduate seminar in the Woodrow Wilson School, where the Professor's wisdom was likely to have been distilled and reproduced. As one who has interested himself in the history of foreign investment in Latin America, I rebel when the sole source for Ralph Harbison's Table 3.7 (' "Nominal" or "Par" Value of British Investments in Colombia') for 1881, 1900 and 1913, is J. F. Rippy, *British Investments in Latin America, 1822–1949* (Minneapolis, 1959), quite the worst of the statistical 'source books' of its generation! Nevertheless, it is all grist to the mill, and from it comes *The Evolution of the International Order* no less, the 'Eliot Janeway Lectures on Historical Economics in honour of Joseph Schumpeter', delivered by Sir Arthur at Princeton in 1977 (and published by the Princeton University Press in 1978). In international circles, Lewis reminded us, 'the topic of the day is the demand of the Third World for a new international economic order', and his lectures suggested urgent and appropriate remedies. But what if he got his numbers wrong?

COLIN CLARK

Lewis's sources are obviously weak, but it would be unfair to single him out; he was not alone. 'World trade', even nowadays, is very largely unquantifiable. When Sir Alexander Cairncross, back in the 1950s, adventured into 'World Trade in Manufactures since 1900', he, like everybody else, quoted *Folke Hilgerdt and the League of Nations, *Arthur Lewis, *H. Tyszynski, *Ingmar Svennilson and the United Nations, and he matched them with 'the new SITC data in order to establish the main trends in world trade in manufactures'. The purpose of Cairncross's paper was to alert economists both to the 'wealth of statistical data now available' and to the manner in which these statistics could be employed.[11]

I would hesitate, myself, before giving the same advice, but it is true that Sir Alexander, Sir Arthur and others were working within a 'world order' of statistics which must have seemed remarkably persuasive at the time. Colin Clark was not strong on facts. His *Conditions of Economic Progress* (1940) was a squirrel's hoard. His British figures began in 1688 (from Gregory King), from which he calculated the growth of real income in Britain since 1401! He printed a table that supposedly illustrated the trend of 'World Trade' at frequent intervals from 1851 to the end of the nineteenth century and then annually from 1900, the source of which, for 1860–1885, was *Neumann-Spallart, other German statistics from 1886, and the *League of Nations from 1913.[12] Subsequent editions of the *Conditions of Economic Progress* were an improvement, although Clark's final 'excursus' in the third 'largely rewritten' edition of 1957 – by which time he was Director of the Institute for Research in Agricultural Economics at Oxford (1953–69) – made economic comparisons with the Ancient World in which, for example, a table was prepared to show the 'average wages per year assuming 300 working days' for Egypt from about 18 BC to the third century AD.[13]

It was good clean fun, but even in the more solemn passages Clark was able to print a table for capital resources and their accumulation (capital expressed as a multiple of net national product) which contained figures for France back to 1789, the UK to 1801, and the United States to 1805.[14]

C. K. HOBSON AND A. H. IMLAH

Britain's international statistics before 1914 are associated with the work of A. H. Imlah. Both figures and method in his *Economic Elements in the Pax Britannica: Studies in British Foreign Trade in the Nineteenth Century* (Cambridge, Mass., 1958) have influenced generations of historians. My objections to Imlah's numbers for Britain's 'Balance of Payments', 1816–1913, are already in print,[15] and I would be repeating myself if I came back to them now – much as I would if I returned to the equally questionable figures for Britain's investment abroad over the century before 1914, where *L. H. Jenks[16] and *Herbert Feis[17] have so long supplied the conventional wisdom.

Imlah's figures for 'British' *trade* are less vulnerable. He understood the common problem with imports (for which only 'official values' were recorded before 1854), and he was able, with the assistance of the published work of others, to make a credible recalculation of imports at real values from 1816. Since Imlah's figures after 1854 are simply those of the Board of Trade, the series is reasonably reliable, bearing in mind the problems that exist with all statistics for foreign trade. C. K. Hobson, on whom Imlah modelled much of his work, had already explained that the Board of Trade had 'both exaggerate[d] and understate[d] the volume of Britain's imports and exports'.[18] Yet this hardly justifies Imlah's claim that his balance of payments series – the most important and most quoted in *Economic Elements* – were 'fairly dependable in . . . measuring the rate and magnitude of British development in these matters during the century'.[19] The use of Stephen Bourne, a retired West Indian magistrate, amateur statistician and author of *The Human Body: an Address* (1865) and *Plain Thoughts on Purity* (1885), as a key source in two of the main statistical series (ship sales and net credits for shipping) is worrying. Bourne felt little need to quote sources. He was a better statistician than *Mulhall, but his *Trade, Population and Food: A Series of Papers on Economic Statistics* (1880) is in the Mulhall tradition.

Imlah, like so many before and since, felt the need to find *some* estimate from which to project his series. In this he followed, rather more than he has since been credited with, the balance of payments 'method' first publicised by C. K. Hobson. Imlah added some portions to Hobson and tidied others, but Hobson, too, enjoyed imaginative extrapolations. For example, he followed a single number in calculating the expenditure for services by the United Kingdom (not in return for exported goods or as payment of interest on capital) over the whole and remarkably diverse period from 1870 to 1912. He had found evidence to suggest, for 1907–1908, a figure of £6 million. If that same proportion, he argued, were applied in 1870, the corresponding figure would be about £3 million. On this basis[20] Hobson calculated *annual* figures back to 1870 and forward to 1912. For a more important table (the income derived by the UK for its services as banker, commission and insurance agent etc., on account of other countries), Hobson accepted Sir Robert Giffen's estimate (*Journal of the Royal Statistical Society*, 1899) of £18 million for the current year. It was this single guess, in proportion to Britain's imports and exports for 1899, that Hobson projected backwards and forwards to 1870 and to 1912.[21]

Hobsonian echoes are strong in Imlah. Hobson was more at home with the calculations for shipping than Imlah, but his coverage in other respects was not so comprehensive. Yet Hobson, like Imlah, drew on inadequate evidence and projected single figures (sometimes *poor* figures) backwards and forwards over a great span of years. The advantage of Hobson (1913) over Imlah (1958) is that Hobson did not pretend to project *his* series as far back as 1816.

SIMON KUZNETS

It may be helpful to take a single example, and to examine it in some depth. The danger is that, whoever is chosen, the accusation will follow that the selection is unrepresentative and probably marginal. But Simon Kuznets was Professor of Political Economy at Johns Hopkins in the 1950s and, in the 1960s, Professor of Economics at Harvard. In 1971 he was awarded the Nobel Prize in Economics both for his pioneering work in comprehensive statistical investigations back for a century or more, and for his calculation of economic growth, defined as an increase in GNP. Alexander Gerschenkron, no less, thought that Kuznets's 'speculations' should be taken as a 'stimulating and challenging program for empirical research'.[22]

Simon Kuznets, like Fernand Braudel, saw the value of argument over the long run (the *longue durée*). In his *Economic Growth of Nations: Total Output and Production Structures* (Cambridge, Mass., 1971) he focused almost entirely on the period after the Second World War. But for the purpose of long-run comparisons (back before 1914) Kuznets took an improbable path – a total output index for England and Wales, gross national income for Great Britain over the decade 1801–1811, net national product for France from 1831–1840, the GDP of Japan 1874–1879.[23] Even when making use of 'developed' countries such as these, among which he included, 'only for illustrative purposes', his few 'less-developed' countries (before 1914), Kuznets arrived at what may appear to be credible numbers and percentages on the basis of what can only be described as the incredible. Thus his first set of 'findings', for developed countries over the long term (from the middle of the eighteenth century), assumed very precise percentages to establish that while population tripled over a century, per capita product rose more than five-fold and total product 'by a factor of at least fifteen over a century' (late eighteenth to late nineteenth centuries)[24] – all of which might indeed depend on the quality of his data for the mid-eighteenth century!

Kuznets's 'findings' stretch on (and on), and the point is that for the long term, back 150 years and on one occasion 'roughly to the early Middle Ages',[25] the numerical base is far too weak either to confirm or deny his conclusions. He was arguing for the 'long sequences of changes in economic and social structure and growth that characterize economic development'. But long sequences require long (and sometimes unlikely) series of figures.

I should explain. Kuznets's sources for pre–1930 figures in *Economic Growth of Nations* (1971) can be traced back to his earlier book, *Modern Economic Growth: Rate, Structure and Spread* (New Haven, Conn., 1966).[26] 'World' population was derived from *M. K. Bennett, *Sir Alexander Carr-Saunders, the *League of Nations, *W. S. and E. S. Woytinsky, *Walter F. Willcox, *Dudley Kirk, *Imre Ferenczi and the *United Nations. It was from these that he drew conclusions based on 'facts', such as the rise of the number of people of 'European stock' by no less than 433 per cent from 1750 to 1950, compared with an increase of less than 200 per cent over the rest of the world. The temptation was too great. Conference papers were in constant demand. At a gathering of the International Economic Association at Bled in the summer of 1970 Kuznets supplied figures which, even for 1965 (the date to which they relate), strain the imagination: one table showed the 'Distribution of World Population by Per Capita Gross Domestic Product (at Market Prices) and by Major Regions, all LDCs included'; another explained 'The Gap: Concept, Measurement, Trends'.[27] Am I unnecessarily cautious in doubting the probability of such figures? They have been reprinted, after all, without further comment or explanation, in Gustav Ranis (ed.), *The Gap Between Rich and Poor Nations* (London, 1972).

Population figures are a notorious trap, but in the circumstances it may not be so extraordinary to find that Kuznets's basic data in other areas were almost as weak. His analysis for 'World Foreign Trade and Its Distribution by Countries, Long Waves, 1720–1958', came first from *Mulhall's *Dictionary*, after which, from 1881 to 1913, it was taken from *Hilgerdt/League of Nations. 'World' trade, 1913 to 1950, was from *Svennilson/United Nations. Kuznets's source for Britain's foreign investment (stock figures for 1874, 1880, 1890, 1900 and 1914) was *Imlah and *Feis, and he relied on the columns in Imlah's balance of payments for profit on foreign trade and services, insurance and brokerage, net shipping credits, interest and dividend balance.[28]

These are curious enough, but they were taken very seriously at the time. In his Chapter 6, 'Trends in International Interdependence', Kuznets again cited Mulhall, this time (even more oddly) for Germany and Italy. His conclusion was that, contrary to what other scholars had said, we now had, on his own figures, a 'firm basis for asserting that trends in the trade proportions of the older developed countries in the period before World War I were generally and significantly upward, not downward'.[29] My *instinct* tells me that this may be right, but the rights and wrongs could not be corroborated from such evidence as Kuznets supplied.

Kuznets's 'Quantitative Aspects of the Economic Growth of Nations; Level and Structure of Foreign Trade: Long-Term Trends' was published in that very holy of holies of econometric history, *Economic Development and Cultural Change* (January 1967). As one might expect, it was dauntingly professional with a theoretical Appendix that guides us, somewhat obscurely, through the 'additive and multiplicative assumptions applied to changes over time'. Its conclusions might be more likely to impress if the numbers to be applied did not include so much of *Mulhall, *Maddison and, especially, *P. Lamartine Yates. From Mulhall's *Dictionary*, for example, Kuznets 'found' that the share of Latin America in foreign trade for the 'rest of the world' (that is, the world less Europe, the United States and Canada) was roughly 0.3 per cent on average for 1870 and 1880. Now, if this share, in turn, were applied to the corresponding total for 1876–1880 supplied by *P. Lamartine Yates. . . .

All the old names recur in one combination or another – *Carr-Saunders, the *Woytinskys, the *League of Nations, the *United Nations, *ECLA, *GATT, *Maizels, *Deane and Cole, *Mitchell and Deane. We must ask: on what basis can the relative importance of foreign trade in the world, from the nineteenth century to the 1960s, be so confidently and precisely proclaimed? How can 'long-term trends in the level and structure of foreign trade' be usefully identified and employed? Foreign trade proportions, even in the relatively prosperous 1920s and 1950s, Kuznets argued, were lower than before the First World War. In 1963 'the foreign trade proportion for the non-Communist world was about a third lower than in 1913'.[30] Well, was it?

A Nobel Prize can preclude further thought; the conference circuit becomes a kind of Monte Carlo Grand Prix. Kuznets was a great figure in international economics, but it is clear that he never felt the need to re-examine numbers sacred since the Nobel celebrations of 1971. Extraordinary figures recur in a 1977 supplement of *Economic Development and Cultural Change*, where he celebrated the 'explosive rise in the flow of basic data on the economic performance and growth of nations'. It is true that the data are much improved, but we are now in the last quarter of the twentieth century, and it was Kuznets himself, after all, who insisted on the importance of the 'long term' and 'historical perspective'. Addressing a United Nations Symposium on Population and Development in June 1973, this time in Cairo, the eminent Laureate found 'particularly helpful' the 'world population' figures of *D. V. Glass in Vol. VI of *The Cambridge Economic History of Europe*.[31] He was indeed hypnotised by figures, particularly 'official' figures, from which he has supplied those 'upper-bound' and 'lower-bound' estimates that delight economists and cliometricians. Yet the base before 1939, and more especially before 1914, may suggest that even upper- and lower-bound figures can support more than a fragment of fantasy.

Notes

1. F. W. Taussig, *International Trade* (New York, 1927) p. vii.
2. *Ibid.*, pp. 245ff.

3. Bertil Ohlin, *Interregional and International Trade* (Cambridge, Mass., 1933) p. x.
4. Gunnar Myrdal, *An International Economy, Problems and Prospects* (London, 1956), Chapter VIII, fn. 4. My doubts are expressed in Platt, *Britain's Investment Overseas on the Eve of the First World War: The Use and Abuse of Numbers* (London, 1986) *passim*.
5. Myrdal, *Asian Drama: An Inquiry into the Poverty of Nations*, Vol.II (Harmondsworth, 1968) p. 1397. His source was United Nations, Department of Social Affairs, Population Division, *The Determinants and Consequences of Population Trends* (New York, 1953) p. 11.
6. Ragnar Nurkse, *Patterns of Trade and Development* (Stockholm, 1959) pp. 19–20, 22, fn. 1.
7. W. Arthur Lewis, *Aspects of Tropical Trade, 1883–1965* (Stockholm, 1969), Statistical Appendix.
8. Lewis, 'World Production, Prices and Trade, 1870–1960', *Manchester School of Economic and Social Studies*, XX:2 (1952).
9. H. Tyszynski, 'World Trade in Manufactured Commodities, 1899–1950', *Manchester School of Economic and Social Studies*, XIX (1951) *passim*.
10. I explain this in more detail in my *Britain's Investment Overseas*, pp. 17–21.
11. A. K. Cairncross, 'World Trade in Manufactures since 1900', *Economia Internazionale*, VIII (1955).
12. Colin Gordon Clark, *The Conditions of Economic Progress* (London, 1940) pp. 459, 461.
13. *Ibid*. (third edn 1957) p. 678.
14. *Ibid*., pp. 574–7.
15. Platt, *Britain's Investment Overseas*, pp. 17–21.
16. L. H. Jenks, *The Migration of British Capital to 1875* (New York, 1927), as examined in Platt, *Foreign Finance in Continental Europe and the USA, 1817–1870: Quantities, Origins, Functions and Distribution* (London, 1984) *passim*.
17. Herbert Feis, *Europe, the World's Banker, 1870–1914* (New Haven, Conn., 1930), as examined in Platt, *Britain's Investment Overseas*, *passim*.
18. C. K. Hobson, *The Export of Capital* (London, 1914) p. 164.
19. Albert H. Imlah, *Economic Elements in the Pax Britannica: Studies in British Foreign Trade in the Nineteenth Century* (Cambridge, Mass., 1958) p. 82.
20. Hobson, *Export of Capital*, pp. 193, 197.
21. *Ibid*., pp. 188, 190.
22. Alexander Gerschenkron was reviewing a publication of the National Bureau of Economic Research, *Demographic and Economic Change in Developed Countries* (Princeton, New Jersey, 1960); the review is reprinted in Gerschenkron, *Continuity in History and Other Essays* (Cambridge, Mass., 1968).
23. Simon Kuznets, *Economic Growth of Nations: Total Output and Production Structure* (Cambridge, Mass., 1971) pp. 11–13.
24. *Ibid*., pp. 303–4.
25. *Ibid*., p. 310.

26. Kuznets, *Modern Economic Growth: Rate, Structure and Spread* (New Haven, Conn., 1966) pp. 35–6, 295–6.
27. Reprinted in Kuznets, *Growth, Population, and Income Distribution: Selected Essays* (New York, 1979).
28. Kuznets, *Modern Economic Growth*, pp. 306–8, 322–5.
29. *Ibid.*, p. 316.
30. Kuznets, 'Quantitative Aspects', p. 70.
31. Reprinted in Kuznets, *Growth, Population, and Income Distribution*.

4 The Moderns

Some overlap exists with the first generation of 'reapers' since, happily, human life spans three score years and ten. But a convenient division is between the 'moderns' – Yates, Maizels, Maddison and Bairoch – and the earlier tradition of the 'Stockholm' group, the Wicksell Lectures, and their heirs. In many, or even most, cases the data are precisely the same.

PAUL LAMARTINE YATES

Lamartine Yates is a name to conjure with in the historiography of international trade. His publishers, warming to their author, describe his book *Forty Years of Foreign Trade* (1959) as the 'long-needed successor to [*Folke Hilgerdt's] *Industrialisation and Foreign Trade*'.[1] The subtitle explains that *Forty Years of Foreign Trade* had 'special reference to Primary Products and Under-Developed Countries'. Yates, like *Hilgerdt, *Nurske, *Svennilson, *Condliffe, *Maddison and *Bairoch, had served an international institution – in *his* case the Food and Agriculture Organisation of the United Nations at Rome. With great industry he prepared his own tabulation of world trade for the key year 1913: 'the exports and imports of ninety-three countries classified into fifty-seven commodity groups, and expressed in a common currency'.[2] The 1953 figures, amplified by Yates himself, came from the Secretariat of the *United Nations. His material for the inter-war years was taken from surveys commissioned by the *League of Nations. His figures for 1876 to 1900 came also from the League of Nations, namely **Industrialisation and Foreign Trade*. He employed *W. A. Lewis's 'World Production, Prices and Trade, 1870–1960', in conjunction with the League's *Industrialization and Foreign Trade*, to construct a series of index numbers of unit values for world trade, manufactures and primary goods separately, from the quinquennium 1876–80.[3]

Yates's contribution – and it was considerable – was to conduct his own census of 'world' trade for 1913, imports and exports; it was a new element in the argument (although, as he admitted, he had not been able to solve the standard problems of valuation, classification, coverage, exchanges, re-exports, etc.). He then brought his own census into an argument founded on data from the *League of Nations and the *United Nations, and built a series of gigantic tables for World Exports of Merchandise (1913–1953), Exports of Primary Products by Regions (1876/80–1953), Manufactured Exports by Regions (1876/80–1953), Primary Products: Imports by Regions, and Manufactured Products: Imports by Regions.[4] His conclusion, on the basis of League of Nations/United Nations data and his own census for 1913, was that:

> In round numbers world trade increased in volume by nearly two-thirds between 1913 and 1953, almost the whole of the increase occurring after World War II. By comparison trade trebled in the forty years *before* 1913.[5]

The snag was Yates's definition of 'world' trade; more critically, it was the extent to which either the League's tables or those of the United Nations were measuring the same thing.

ALFRED MAIZELS

Alfred Maizels's *Industrial Growth of World Trade: 1899–1959* (1963), an 'empirical study', was published under the auspices of the National Institute of Economic and Social Research. When he retreated into the remoter past, he normally used the figures of the main European countries, the United States, Britain's white dominions, and India; with reservations, it should be possible from the export statistics of this particular group of nations to assemble a respectable base figure. When, however, Maizels moved on to 'world' trade (Chapter 4), one of his tables indicated 'world trends in population, production and trade, 1876–1959', while others, in the Appendix, give us impossible numbers like those for the imports of manufactures *per capita* of Brazil and Mexico in 1899 and 1913. And what is to be made of precise broken-down figures (1899 and 1913) for the imports into Argentina, Brazil, Chile and Colombia, Japan, Mexico, Turkey and the USSR?[6] The sources, for the period up to 1914, were the *League of Nations' *Industrialization and Foreign Trade* and *W. A. Lewis's first article of 1952. Maizels's world trade figures for 1913 were from *P. Lamartine Yates, while *Lewis was employed for pre-1914 data elsewhere.[7]

These were not on their own. Table E1 supplied estimates of GDP for selected countries 1899–1957, the Latin American component of which came from *ECLA's *Economic Development of Argentina*. The same sources were given for Table E2 ('estimates of gross domestic product per head of population for selected countries 1899–1957') and for Table E4 ('estimates of net volume of manufacturing production per head of total population in selected countries, 1899–1957'). It continued in the same vein, and we are offered a table E7 for 'total population of selected countries, 1899–1957' which, among other unlikely numbers, gave the population of Argentina, Brazil, Chile, Cuba and Mexico for 1899, although Colombia, Peru and Puerto Rico had to wait until 1913. Maizels himself gave no precise references for this information, but it was taken most probably from the *League of Nations' *Statistical Yearbooks* or the *Demographic Yearbooks* of the United Nations.

The suspicion must be that similar standards were employed in Maizels's later work, *Exports and Economic Growth of Developing Countries: a Theoretical and Empirical Study of the Relationship between Exports and Economic Growth* (Cambridge, 1965). Maizels computed shares of 'more developed countries' and 'less developed countries' (Africa, South and South-East Asia), country by country, for 1953–55 and 1960–61. By now Maizels could draw on the much improved data published by the United Nations in its *Yearbook of International Trade Statistics*. But a similar range of calculations for the years *before* the First World War, and indeed for 'less developed countries' over much of the 1920s and 1930s, is absurd.

ANGUS MADDISON

In chapter 5 I shall describe the numerical base in 'world history' of cliometrics. In Chapter 6 I do the same for Braudel's disciples of the 'development school'. Meanwhile, I refer to the more conventional approach of Angus Maddison, Phyllis Deane and W. A. Cole, and Paul Bairoch.

I have mentioned already that Maddison belongs to the category of international civil servant that produced, among others, *Hilgerdt, *Svennilson and *Yates. From 1953 Maddison was employed by the Organisation for European Economic Cooperation and Development; he became head of the Economics division in 1958 and Director of the Development Department in 1963. His experience was that of working within an international organisation, and it may not be unfair to say, on the analogy of what I suggest for the *League of Nations and the *United Nations, that the temptation at this level is to take the first likely (and available) figure in an otherwise unfamiliar area, without digging too deep. The attitude is entirely understandable. Unfamiliar areas ('world' statistics before the Second World War) are a mere prelude to more sophisticated analyses from 1945. The problem comes when such notional figures, introduced for limited ends, are given status and trust by subsequent generations.

Maddison's background in the OECD must account for the close interest he displays in 'world' trade. His articles in the *Quarterly Review* of the Banca Nazionale del Lavoro are widely cited. 'Growth and Fluctuation in the World Economy, 1870–1960', *Quarterly Review* 15 (1962), drew its earlier figures for 'world trade' from *Hilgerdt's *Industrialization and Foreign Trade*, which in turn cited *Neumann-Spallart; other 'world' data (exports and imports) came from *Lewis's *Manchester School* article of May 1952. GNP figures (in any practical sense, inaccessible) were nonetheless supplied from the 1870s for Denmark, Germany, Italy, Sweden, the United Kingdom, 'Western Europe' (others) and Canada, and from 1889 for the United States. Maddison was able to conclude that 'the annual increase in volume [of 'world' trade] for 1950–60 was 6.4 per cent as compared with 3.4 per cent from 1870 to 1913, and about 1 per cent in 1913–38.[8]

It was Maddison's article in the *Quarterly Review* (1962) that became the base ('unless otherwise specified') for the estimates, 1870–1950, repeated in his book of twenty years later, *Phases of Capitalist Development* (Oxford, 1982).[9] Much had been published in the interval, but it is curious that in 'world' trade (exports and imports back to 1720) the 'basic source for most estimates' had regressed to *Mulhall's *Dictionary*. Mulhall, Maddison admits, did not actually give sources, but no matter since 'his aggregate was used by eminent contemporaries', while *Kuznets and *W. W. Rostow's *The World Economy* had employed them more recently.[10] Reassured, Maddison constructed his own world export volume index for intervals between 1720 and 1970, comparing it with Rostow's (Mulhall's) world trade volume index from 1720 to 1913.

Maddison's *Phases of Capitalist Development* does not pretend to be the product of original research. Although he realised the weakness of some of these estimates, 'particularly for years before 1913', this did not in practice prevent him from producing 'movement in GDP' figures for France and Britain periodically from 1700, and for most European countries from the mid-nineteenth century; Japan's

GDP, with an 'interpolation' for 1870, was quoted from 1885.[11] For Britain he is on more solid ground with *Phyllis Deane and *Charles Feinstein. But GDP figures remain elusive, and the suggestion that the foreign assets of the United Kingdom were 1.5 times as high as GDP, or that income from foreign property in 1913 accounted for the fact that GNP was 9.4 per cent higher than GDP, is less convincing when, as it seems, the source for the United Kingdom's foreign assets (£3.8 billion) was *Herbert Feis.[12]

Phases of Capitalist Development dealt broadly with a vast range of information, and it is obviously the more successful the closer it approaches the present day. The difficulty, as always, has been the doubtful quality of the information for earlier periods and the deductions and comparisons that follow. Maddison is an economist. As an economist he remarks that the foreign assets of the United States in 1976 were equal to less than a fifth of GDP – which may or may not be true at the time he was writing (I am not qualified to say). But he then concludes that 'this is less than a fifteenth of the Dutch 1790 ratio or a seventh of that of the UK in 1914'. Maddison's source for Dutch finance was J. C. Riley, *International Government Finance and the Amsterdam Capital Market 1740–1815* (Cambridge, 1980). Riley's calculations were confined simply to loans for foreign governments, and made no allowance for the private sector or for direct investment in a semi-public enterprise like the Dutch East India Company. Maddison's estimate of Holland's national income for 1792 came from 'Metelerkamp', referred to unhelpfully as such in H. C. Bos's mimeographed paper, 'Economic Growth in the Netherlands', published in 1959.[13]

What is 'world' trade? Maddison's 'world', before 1914, meant sixteen countries. For these sixteen, the 'annual average compound growth rates' on the value of exports, 1720–1820, were calculated on three countries alone; these rose to ten countries for 1820–1870 and sixteen thereafter (the figures for which, including the Hapsburg Empire, were 'not adjusted for changes in geographic boundaries').[14] Now, *what* is this supposed to mean?

PHYLLIS DEANE AND W. A. COLE

*B. R. Mitchell's *Abstract of British Historical Statistics* (1962), prepared in collaboration with Phyllis Deane, was simply a collection of digested statistics. Phyllis Deane and W. A. Cole, *British Econ-*

omic Growth 1688–1959: Trends and Structure (Cambridge, 1962), was more deductive. Like *Charles Feinstein's *National Income, Expenditure and Output of the United Kingdom, 1855–1965* (Cambridge, 1971), it focused on domestic issues; it has become a major source for the economic development of Britain at home. The problems lie abroad.

Table 83 ('Growth in volume of international trade and national income in the nineteenth century') based its trade figures on *Imlah's volume indices, taking Deane and Cole's own national income estimates. My opinion on Imlah's methods is given elsewhere, and the national income estimates have the difficulties spelt out by the authors themselves for Table 72 ('The national product of Great Britain in the nineteenth century').[15] From these, alas, we have broad and debatable generalisations for the influence of foreign trade in 'setting the pace for British economic growth' to the First World War, followed by others such as the conclusion, from net foreign investment (taken from *Imlah), that up to the beginning of the First World War 'the United Kingdom's earnings from its foreign assets were more than sufficient to finance the passive balance of merchandise trade'.[16] Disappointingly, there is no full or even partial discussion of *Imlah's method.

PAUL BAIROCH

Like *Maddison, Paul Bairoch, professor at the University of Geneva, had worked for an international agency (GATT); his strength, consequently, lay in the 'official' material he gathered from the agencies for the years after the Second World War. Bairoch's *Commerce extérieur du Tiers-Monde* first appeared in Paris in 1967, and in 1976 a further *Commerce extérieur et développement économique de l'Europe au XIX*e *siècle* was released under the sponsorship of the École des Hautes Études en Sciences Sociales. During the 1970s Bairoch published a series of influential articles in the *Journal of European Economic History*.[17] He shares the distaste of *Gunnar Myrdal and *Raúl Prebisch for the liberal economics of comparative advantage; he too is an enthusiast for autarchy in the less-developed world. It is all very well meant, strongly argued and unequivocally maintained. But it has little contact with historical 'method'.

The alarm is sounded early in the extensive literature, and no doubt Bairoch's assumptions have the gloss of public service. There is no need to analyse the pattern of foreign trade for each individual, Bairoch explained in his *Economic Development of the Third World since 1900* (the translated edition of *Commerce extérieur du Tiers-Monde*), as 'complete and reliable statistics are available for the Third World as a whole'.[18] At this point, when Bairoch's real interest was in the figures for after 1938, he was content to refer simply to 'author's estimates' (unexplained) for his data before 1914, although it appears that he reached them by way of revised figures from the *League of Nations, *C. P. Kindleberger, and *Maizels. It is from these that he can confidently conclude that overseas trade formed about 16 per cent of world trade in 1900, and had reached 19 per cent by 1913.[19]

Bairoch presented more ambitious 'world' analyses in his articles for the *Journal of European Economic History*. It is unnecessary to follow these through in depth, and it may be sufficient to explain that he depended for international trade statistics in the nineteenth century on *Mulhall, particularly on Mulhall's *Industries and Wealth of Nations* (London, 1886) and the fourth edition of the *Dictionary of Statistics* (London, 1898). As for Europe generally, Bairoch was confident that the statistical coverage, 1880–1913, was 100 per cent![20] His figures for before the First World War, in later articles, came additionally from *Svennilson/United Nations, and the sources for his 1974 article included, besides *Mulhall, *McCulloch, and *von Neumann-Spallart, the 'official' figures published in that neutral guide, the *Statesman's Yearbook*. The third of Bairoch's articles (in the *Journal of European Economic History* for 1976) is a development, slightly revised, of *Maddison's 'Growth and Fluctuation in the World Economy, 1870–1960' in which , among other curiosities, Bairoch gave estimates of European GDP, 1800–1913, and later compared his results with *Colin Clark's data in *The Conditions of Economic Progress*.[21]

More recently, in 1982, Bairoch published a fourth article in the *Journal of European Economic History* on international industrialisation, 1750–1980.[22] For the nineteenth century he again used *Mulhall's *Industries and Wealth of Nations* (1886), while *Maizels and *Lewis supported his story through to 1913. But this was an article that ranged well beyond the Europe to which the others were limited, and it included, from 'author's computations and estimates', figures for total 'world' production and 'world' population from 1750 – by which the 'world's' per capita production might be derived.

Much of the origin of this miscellany is explained in the 'annexe méthodologique et statistique' of Bairoch's *Commerce extérieur et développement économique*. On the basis of the figures he produced, it is impossible to confirm his views on when and where, if at all, foreign trade became the 'moteur d'expansion économique'; nor can one establish the rights and wrongs of free trade versus protection in economic development world-wide. Bairoch's readers, unfortunately, are likely to take this more seriously than it deserves. The 'annexe méthodologique' of the first part of Bairoch's next book, *Taille des villes, conditions de vie et développements économiques* (Paris, 1977), shows again how dependent he had become on the figures, historical or otherwise, of the *United Nations.

GENERALISTS: S. B. SAUL, A. J. BROWN, H. MYINT AND L. J. ZIMMERMAN

If the specialists can get it so wrong, the generalists and textbook writers are unlikely to prove much better. *Lamartine Yates surfaces as the source for S. B. Saul's analysis of the relative importance of Britain in primary products (which fell sharply, it seems, from 'about 30 per cent in 1876–80 to 19 per cent in 1913'), while *Maizels supplied the figures for French, British and German manufactured exports, 1899–1913. *Tyszynski was the origin of Saul's Table V: 'World Exports of Manufactured Goods (percentage shares) of the United Kingdom, the United States, France, Germany, Belgium and Japan for 1899 and 1913', and also of Table IV. Table VII came from *Maizels and Table IX from both *Maizels and *Tyszynski.[23]

A. J. Brown's *Introduction to the World Economy* (1959), which became a popular textbook in the 1960s, was unfootnoted. But there is good reason to doubt his propositions that 'Britain in 1851 was the source of between a quarter and a third of all the goods which were sent across international frontiers', that 'the volume of manufactured output in the world trebled between 1870 and 1900', and finally that 'world trade has never been so high in relation to world income as it was in 1914'.[24]

*Lamartine Yates is cited yet again as the origin for the notion, quoted in H. Myint's *The Economics of Developing Economies* (many editions in the 1970s, and again in 1980), that, contrary to general impression, African and Latin American countries 'expanded the total value of their exports ten-fold during the years 1913–1935'.[25]

But it is L. J. Zimmermann, professor at the Institute of Social Studies at the Hague, who outdoes them all. When describing the 'distribution of world income, 1860–1960', Zimmermann felt that although there were problems with the data even for developed countries in the nineteenth century, 'we think, nevertheless, that the estimates for North America, Oceania, North West Europe, the Soviet Union, Japan and South East Asia are rather reliable'. As for Latin America and the Far East, Zimmermann made his own estimates 'based mainly on the trends we found in other areas'. His figures included *per capita* income for Latin America and China from 1850, from which he discovered 'the first amazing – and for ourselves completely unexpected – result', i. e. the 'constant and rather high increase in the average world income' coupled with increased inequality in its distribution.

As with Bairoch, it is all very well meant, and Professor Zimmermann's 'findings' may have amazed others less than they did himself. But however did he reach, in his own estimates, precise population figures for 'Latin America' and China in 1860 and 1913? His calculations include the income of the 'median world citizen' in 1860, from which he confidently argued that the income distribution between the various parts of the world was becoming ever less equal, 'which is demonstrated by using the so-called Lorenz curves'. Zimmermann then computed the 'Pareto coefficient' for the whole period 1860–1959 from which, it seems, it is further demonstrated that one hundred years ago (in never-never land) 'the distribution of the world income was much more equal than it is today'. The decline, he agreed, will surely 'inaugurate a revolutionary situation'.[26] Zimmermann's 'Statistical Appendix' reveals complete confusion – heavy reliance on *United Nations publications of one kind or another, random pickings elsewhere, and, for Latin America, an entirely inadequate base.

Notes

1. P. Lamartine Yates, *Forty Years of Foreign Trade* (London, 1959).
2. *Ibid.*, p. 9.
3. *Ibid.*, pp. 201–4.

4. *Ibid.*, pp. 224–30.
5. *Ibid.*, p. 10.
6. Alfred Maizels, *Industrial Growth of World Trade: An Empirical Study of Trends in Production, Consumption and Trade from 1899–1959* (Cambridge, 1963) pp. 443 and 455ff.
7. *Ibid.*, pp. 80, 107 and 108. *Lewis was cited generally for data from before the First World War, for example in Table 4:3 (p. 88).
8. Angus Maddison, 'Growth and Fluctuation in the World Economy, 1870–1960', Banca Nazionale del Lavoro, *Quarterly Review*, 61 (1962) p. 127.
9. Angus Maddison, *Phases of Capitalist Development* (Oxford, 1982), Appendix F.
10. *Ibid.*, p. 254.
11. *Ibid.*, pp. 169ff (Appendix A).
12. *Ibid.*, p. 259, fn. 18.
13. *Ibid.*, p. 258, fn. 10.
14. *Ibid.*, p. 60.
15. Phyllis Deane and W. A. Cole, *British Economic Growth 1688–1959: Trends and Structure* (Cambridge, 2nd edn 1967) pp. 311–12.
16. *Ibid.*, pp. 36–7, and see the use of *Imlah's estimates of Britain's foreign investment on p. 265 and his estimates of net income from abroad on p. 297.
17. Paul Bairoch, 'European Foreign Trade in the XIX Century: the Development of the Volume and Value of Exports (Preliminary Results)', *Journal of European Economic History*, 2:1 (Spring 1973); also 'Geographical Structure and Trade Balance of European Foreign Trade from 1800 to 1970', *JEEH*, 3:3 (Winter 1974); and 'Europe's Gross National Product: 1800–1975', *JEEH*, 5:2 (Fall 1976).
18. Bairoch, *The Economic Development of the Third World since 1900* (London, 1975) p. 92.
19. *Ibid.*, p. 93.
20. Bairoch, 'European Foreign Trade in the Nineteenth Century', pp. 30, 32.
21. Bairoch, 'Europe's Gross National Product', *passim*.
22. Bairoch, 'International Industrialization Levels from 1750 to 1980', *Journal of European Economic History*, 11:2 (Spring 1982).
23. S. B. Saul, 'The Export Economy, 1870–1914', *Yorkshire Bulletin of Economic and Social Research*, 17:1 (May 1965), *passim*.
24. A. J. Brown, *Introduction to the World Economy* (London, 1959) pp. 145, 147 and 148.
25. H. Myint, *The Economics of Developing Countries* (fifth edn, London 1980) p. 22.
26. L. J. Zimmermann, 'The Distribution of World Income, 1860–1960' in Egbert de Vries (ed.) *Essays on Unbalanced Growth: A Century of Disparity and Convergence* (The Hague, 1962) *passim*.

5 Econometrics

Whether this category is to be described as 'econometrics', 'cliometrics' or, in one peculiar formulation, 'counterfactual history', the reliance on numbers, *any* numbers, is necessarily high. 'A mass of factual research', Gerschenkron reminded us, 'must be carried out before counterfactual questions can be asked'; he did not deny the value of counterfactual history – the assessment of events and results by what might have been – but his qualification was that it should be 'suitably applied'.[1] And the claims of the cliometric 'school' are reasonable enough for the more quantifiable elements like railways, trade, prices, commerce and labour – in fact for *any* activity where numbers are recorded and preserved. It is no small matter, Donald McCloskey argued, to be able to say that economic change in the nineteenth century was *not* utterly dominated by railways, or that the tariff was *not* the 'magic key to economic change in German-speaking Europe'.[2] And there can be nothing but gain from the application of 'serious' economic and statistical analysis, the resistance to which, as Gerschenkron says, might simply be 'inadequate comprehension of the nature of the tools used'.[3]

I should explain that Gerschenkron was writing in 1965 when cliometrics were in their first bloom. He gave them a decade or two before diminishing returns set in.[4] Gerschenkron's deadline has long since passed, and the cliometric 'school' is still very much alive. But its continued existence must depend on the availability of reliable data, as it must equally for such recent refinements in economic history as 'the new institutional economics'.[5]

THE PRACTITIONERS: BIRNBERG, RESNICK AND HANSON II

'World' history has a fatal attraction for the 'number-cruncher'. It would be unkind to multiply the references, but I propose, simply by way of illustration, to examine just two of the more recent books, econometrically inclined, on the history of the Third World.

Thomas B. Birnberg and Stephen A. Resnick, *Colonial Development: An Econometric Study* (New Haven, Conn., 1975), was a publication of Yale's Economic Growth Center. The methods employed were impeccably econometric. However, the sources, from 1850 to 1900, fall short of the ideal. They consisted, in the main, of contemporary 'official' publications, the *League of Nations,* Deane and Cole, *B. R. Mitchell and the *Statesman's Year Book*. Lesser contributions were acknowledged from *J. Fred Rippy, *Herbert Feis, *André Gunder Frank, *L. H. Jenks, *Jonathan Levin and *Aníbal Pinto.

John Hanson's *Trade in Transition* (1980) attempted to describe 'Third World' exports for the second half of the nineteenth century.[6] Hanson, an economist from Texas A & M, has a high regard for the conventional statistical sources. Yet his 'non-Western schema' led him to prefer figures taken directly from the Third World; he suspected that a metropolitan provenance might misrepresent true numbers in the interest of the more advanced trading partners.[7] The argument is laboured, and there is much heavy breathing as Hanson relates the abominable behaviour of the developed nations. His piece was published in a series entitled 'Studies in Social Discontinuity', which sounds about right. But it is feeble stuff, and in calling attention to *Trade in Transition* my purpose is simply to illustrate a common tendency to take 'official' figures for granted in pursuit of 'world' – or, even worse, 'Third World' – history. Perhaps only a 'committed' economist could fall for so simple a trap. Gerschenkron, speaking *de haut en bas*, could afford to be generous when he reminded us, in defence of the eager young counterfactual historians of the 1960s, that it was, after all, their day, and 'its splendour should be neither beclouded nor begrudged'.[8]

THE PROFESSIONALS (I): DOUGLASS C. NORTH AND ROBERT PAUL THOMAS

Sophisticated econometricians take greater care with their figures. Yet the temptation to use *any* number, good or bad, in ever more elaborate econometric games is, if anything, increased.

Douglass C. North and Robert Paul Thomas, in their new economic history of the Western world, had intended to write a 'revolutionary book', revolutionary in the sense that they claimed to have developed a 'comprehensive analytical framework to examine and explain the rise of the Western World: a framework consistent with and complementary to standard neo-classical economic theory'.[9] It was, as they promised, free from the 'jargon of the profession', but the 'revolution' may not have been quite as they hoped. Thorold Rogers, a respected but remote authority, was their source for British wheat prices 1261–1400. The population of Europe 1200–1550 came, astonishingly, from *M. K. Bennett. The figures for Spain in the Golden Age (and before) were those of an economic historian of the old era, Jaime Vicens Vives. Other sources were deeply conventional, like Slicher van Bath's *The Agrarian History of Western Europe: AD 500–1850* (London, 1963).

The Rise of the Western World (1973) and the North and Thomas article of 1970 (its precursor and herald)[10] put forward some interesting ideas, but these lacked a solid base. In the circumstances one wonders (with the Emeritus Professor of Economic History at Cambridge) what purpose is served by such 'bold abstractions over 10,000 years of human history', where the longer the period, the greater the uncertainty, so that it all becomes but a 'highly imaginative piece of intellectual fun'.[11]

THE PROFESSIONALS (II): IRVING B. KRAVIS AND N. F. R. CRAFTS

On a less ambitious, although dauntingly professional, scale was the dispute between Kravis and Crafts over 'world' trade and growth. Again, I am quoting it simply as an example of what may happen over a much larger constituency.

Irving B. Kravis, in an article for the *Economic Journal* of December 1970, argued the case against *Nurkse.[12] His own evidence, he explained, did not support any 'simple generalisation about the dominant role of trade in the success stories of nineteenth-century growth'; he himself preferred 'handmaiden' to 'engine' as a more accurate description of what actually took place.

The argument is immaterial. I need ask only on what it was based. The sources for the sixty years before 1914 in Kravis's Table I ('Percentage Changes per Decade in the Volume of World Trade, Selected Countries, 1820–1966') were as follows: *R. Nurkse, *Equilibrium and Growth in the World Economy*, *Simon Kuznets, 'Quantitative Aspects of the Economic Growth of Nations' and *Angus Maddison, 'Growth and Fluctuation in the World Economy'. After 1929 Kravis used *GATT, *Trends in International Trade* and GATT's *Annual on International Trade*. Similarly, the base for Table II ('Development of World Exports of Primary Products and Manufactures, Originating in Developed and Underdeveloped Areas, 1876/80–1966') was *Paul Lamartine Yates, as it was again for Tables A-19, A-21 and A-23. And Yates was further employed for calculating rates of growth quinquenially 1876/80 to 1913 and similarly from 1913 to 1953.[13]

Kravis was surely right that the rôle of foreign trade has been much exaggerated, and perhaps, since his article (1970) is very much a 'think-piece' taken from secondary material, it may be unreasonable to ask him to verify his sources. But instinct apart, Kravis's ideas cannot be confirmed from the sources he employed, nor may they properly serve as the base for academic dispute. The Kravis/Crafts engagement is a classic example of sophisticated argument deduced from imperfect numbers. N. F. R. Crafts, equally cavalier in his use of numbers, challenged Kravis. But he himself used *Maddison's article of 1962 for Table I (growth rates of exports by value for 'Third Countries' 1876/80–1911/13), and again for Table II ('trade expansion by volume of LDCs 1876/80–1911/13'; he did not question the source.[14]

It would be pleasant to report that this was merely the level of sophistry to be expected from furious debate. Yet a decade later both *Maddison and *Mulhall were *still* cited. The argument in Crafts's chapter on 'Specialization and International Trade' is not perfectly clear, but it seems (*British Economic Growth*, 1985) that *Maddison was the origin of the notion that the 'soon to be developed' countries grew at about 2 per cent per annum from 1815, compared with a rate of much less than 1 per cent in the eighteenth century. *Mulhall was taken to be sufficient to confirm that Britain's share of world trade 'remained fairly constant'.[15] Crafts then constructed a handsome equation, crossing the page from side to side, from which he argued that export-demand growth in the period after the Napoleonic Wars was a 'much more favourable element [in the economic development of the United Kingdom] than earlier' – which is common sense, of course, but which could not possibly be determined either way from figures of the quality employed. Crafts's numbers can often be much better. He used *Maizels for a table that showed the 'Destination of Manufactured Exports in 1913', and this, since it was based on British, United States and Western European government statistics, is reasonably reliable.[16] He added *Tyszynski as the source for revealed comparative advantage in manufacturing, 1913 and 1937, for the United Kingdom, the United States and France, for which much the same can be said.[17] For an historian, however, the presence of good and bad cheek by jowl, without discrimination or comment, is unnerving.

I come finally to a recent paper of the same econometric *genre* – Crafts and Mark Thomas on 'Comparative Advantage in the UK Manufacturing Trade, 1910–1935'. The paper's target is Bela Balassa, great 'pensador' in underdevelopment economics, Professor of Political Economy at Johns Hopkins and consultant to the World Bank. Balassa had declared, conventionally, that before the Second World War developed countries exported goods that were human and physical-capital-intensive (sic) while importing goods that were unskilled-labour-intensive.[18] Crafts and Thomas argued that this had not been the case for the United Kingdom, where 'net exports were positively related to raw labour inputs and negatively related to human capital inputs'.[19]

The approach is characteristic. Balassa was picked up at his weakest point (historical evidence) to serve an impenetrable argument in econometrics. Great sophistication was shown, but the danger signals were all there. For example, Crafts and Thomas employed 'a modification of Leamer's preferred procedure for empirical estimation of factor endowments within the Hecksher – Ohlin framework'. They then quoted *Tyszynski as the source of their Table 4, in which comparative advantage for the United Kingdom, Germany and the United States was calculated, measured as each country's share in 'world' exports and divided by its overall share in 'world' imports.[20] This was then put down solemnly as 'taken from world trade [actually for eleven countries] on 16 broad commodity groups collected by Tyszynski', and calculated by 'Balassa's measure of revealed comparative advantage for British exports in certain benchmark years', all of which, after further figures from *Yates and the Deutsches Reichsamt (1937), was intended to reinforce the view of Britian's decline.[21]

Crafts and Thomas may (or may not) be right that Britain's comparative advantage lay in 'unskilled-labour-intensive, capital-neutral, and human-capital-scarce commodities' (phew!). The profile may (or may not) have remained stable throughout the period from 1870 to 1935.[22] But they have drawn very heavily on *Lamartine Yates's 'classic study',[23] and I personally would prefer to look at those figures again.

Back in the 1920s *Jacob Viner was already objecting to new fashions among economists – fashions that caught up with economic historians only forty years later. The statisticians, he warned, were the 'fanatic advocates of exclusively quantitative economics', and there was virtue in the systematic development of factual information. But he thought, and had done so for years, that there would be many problems in traditional economics that would 'wholly resist quantitative inquiry', and many years before economists, even for themes for which data existed, would learn how to handle analysis. Viner explained that 'the adequately cautious neoclassical economist [had] never laid claim to the possession of sufficient information about his curves to enable him to fit equations to them'.[24] Sixty years later that caution seems largely to have been forgotten.

Notes

1. Alexander Gerschenkron, 'Some Problems in Economic History', in Gerschenkron, *Continuity in History and Other Essays* (Cambridge, Mass., 1968) p. 55.
2. Donald McCloskey, 'The Achievements of the Cliometric School', *Journal of Economic History*, 38 (1978) pp. 24–5.
3. Gerschenkron, 'Some Problems in Economic History', p. 56.
4. *Ibid.*
5. Explained by Kanshik Basu, Eric Jones and Ekkehart Schlicht, 'The Growth and Decay of Custom: The Role of the New "Institutional Economics" in Economic History', *Explorations in Economic History*, 24:1 (January 1987) pp. 1–21.
6. John Hanson II, *Trade in Transition: Exports from the Third World, 1840–1900* (New York, 1980).
7. *Ibid.*, pp. 2–3.
8. Gerschenkron, 'Some Problems in Economic History', p. 56.
9. Douglass C. North and Robert Paul Thomas, *The Rise of the Western World: A New Economic History* (Cambridge, 1973) p. vii.
10. North and Thomas, 'An Economic Theory of the Growth of the Western World', *Economic History Review*, XXIII, 2nd series, 1 (1970) pp. 1–17.
11. D. C. Coleman, *History and the Economic Past: An Account of the Rise and Decline of Economic History in Britain* (Oxford, 1987) p. 133.
12. Irving B. Kravis, 'Trade as a Handmaiden of Growth: Similarities between the Nineteenth and Twentieth Centuries', *Economic Journal*, 80:2 (December, 1970).
13. *Ibid.*, pp. 859–62.
14. N. F. R. Crafts, 'Trade as a Handmaiden of Growth: An Alternative View', *Economic Journal*, 83 (September 1973).

15. Crafts, *British Economic Growth during the Industrial Revolution* (London, 1985) p.151.
16. *Ibid.*, p. 163 (Table 8.3).
17. *Ibid.*, p. 162 (Table 8.2).
18. Bela Balassa, *The Newly-Industrializing Countries in the World Economy* (New York, 1981) pp. 154–5, 164–5.
19. N. F. R. Crafts and Mark Thomas, 'Comparative Advantage in the UK Manufacturing Trade, 1910–1935', *Economic Journal*, 96 (September 1986).
20. *Ibid.*, p. 639.
21. *Ibid.*, pp. 639–40.
22. *Ibid.*, p. 643.
23. *Ibid.*, p. 640.
24. Jacob Viner, 'The Present Status and Future Prospects of Quantitative Economics' (1928), reprinted in Viner, *The Long View and the Short: Studies in Economic Theory and Policy* (Glencoe, Illinois, 1958) p. 43.

6 The 'World System'

It is a misfortune for the great Fernand Braudel, honorary graduand of some twenty of the world's universities and proud holder of the highest honours of France, that his 'geohistory' has given birth to what must surely be the most fanciful of manipulations in historical statistics, the product of the 'development school' of historians.

Fernand Braudel's *longue durée* and the long run of *Simon Kuznets have much in common; both Braudel and Kuznets argued the importance, in history, of taking the long view. Braudel, in applying *la longue durée* to the Mediterranean in the sixteenth century, had no real statistics at his finger tips. What he did was to employ his own wide reading to paint a great canvas. Sir Geoffrey Elton describes him, not unjustly, as 'the last of the "literary" (i. e. not very scholarly) historians to gain academic respect'; he had 'come too soon to employ econometric techniques and refined social science models in the victory of *structure* over *événement*'.[1]

It was Kuznets, then, who won a Nobel Prize because he was, after all, a social 'scientist' and the prize was in economics. Kuznets could not avoid (indeed, he courted) statistics, good and bad indiscriminately, from which he might hope to establish those 'long sequences of changes in economic and social structure and growth that characterise modern economic development'.[2] And long sequences required long (and sometimes improbable) series of figures. The decision to go beyond the short span, said Braudel, was 'the most precious, because the most rare, of historiographical achievements during the past hundred years'. Gibbon and Macaulay had taken challenging themes over huge periods: they had been

> attentive to the perspectives of the longue durée in a way in which, afterwards, only a few great spirits – Michelet, Ranke, Jacob Burckhardt, Fustel [and, by implication, Braudel himself] were able to recapture.[3]

FERNAND BRAUDEL

Fernand Braudel – although he could deploy few numbers for the sixteenth century – confessed himself to be a 'great believer in the usefulness of long sequences of statistics'. He found the whole of eighteenth-century Europe riddled with the workings of statistically minded historians, 'but they crop up even in the seventeenth, and even more in the sixteenth century', while China's population statistics went back an unbelievably long way to the Ming dynasty.[4]

Now, it is probably true that Braudel's statistics – when (infrequently) he took the trouble to supply them – are better than most. Braudel had an eye for the weaker elements, whether they came within or without his professional range. Although described as their 'founding father', Braudel is unlikely ever to have reached the broad conclusions of subsequent 'global' historians.

But there are dangers in the *longue durée* even for a scholar of standing, and still more for its less talented practitioners. It is sad that Braudel himself was ever persuaded to engage in *Les Structures du Quotidien: Le Possible et l'Impossible* (Paris, 1974), published in translation as three great volumes under the title *Civilisation and Capitalism, 15th to 18th Centuries*. The first volume took account of 'world' population, the second 'world' trade, and the third 'world' economics. *Les Structures du Quotidien* is too much of an historical jumble to serve as a reliable base for generalisation on the past, present and future of capitalism. As Braudel himself charmingly admitted in the conclusion to his first volume, 'books, even history books, run away with their authors. This one has run on ahead of me.'[5]

All the same, Braudel's *méthode* is important if only because, for reasons good and bad, it has been immensely influential. Braudel, with some justice, agreed that real numbers do not exist for the history of world population. He rejected the *Woytinskys and had little time for the 'Berkeley School' (S. F. Cook and Woodrow Borah) who, he rightly complained, 'deduced a total for the whole of America from partial Mexican statistics'. Yet Braudel was prepared himself to chart world population from the thirteenth to the nineteenth century, comparing China and Europe and citing some of the great names of nineteenth-century amateur demography. He ridiculed (successfully) the figures for 'world population, 1650–1950' in *Carr-Saunders, *Kuczynski and the *United Nations, but he felt able, after chopping and changing the conventional wisdom, to supply a total for world population in 1680 of 35–50 million for 'Africa', 240–360 million for 'Asia', 100 million for 'Europe', 10 million for 'America' and 2 million for 'Oceania'.[6]

This is all very well. It is an improvement (being more broadly based) on the numbers proposed by the United Nations. But it is still at far remove from any kind of certainty – which would hardly matter if Braudel's acolytes (and Braudel himself) did not take such 'data' too seriously. 'World' population when Braudel was writing (the early 1970s) was 'about' four billion. Comparing his 'very approximate figures' for the past, Braudel calculated that 'world' population was now five times the population of 1800, and twelve times that of 1300:

> These coefficients of 1 to 5 or 1 to 12, with all the values in between, are not magic numbers that explain everything – especially since they refer to realities which are not exactly the same – far from it. However, a comparison of the overall figure alone can open some perspectives for us.[7]

By this Braudel meant phenomena like the small size of towns and armies before the nineteenth century, the relative over-population/under-population of different countries (and the consequences), and the level of civilisation, discovery and settlement.

These are huge themes, but 'perspectives' should open only if the 'overall figure' is credible. As it was, Braudel's calculations were based on a 'world' population of 350 million in 1300 and 1,000 million for 1800.[8] His map (on a two-page spread) showing 'Civilisations, "Cultures" and Primitive Peoples, *c.* 1500' was taken entirely from G. W. Hewes, 'A conspectus of the world's cultures in 1500 AD', to be found only by the most assiduous researcher in *University of Colorado Studies*, No. 4 (1954). It is from Hewes, then, that Braudel set about constructing general arguments like the 'mistake' made by Europe when it thought that it alone had discovered a New World.[9]

There is a limit to what we can take, and Braudel's ideas have at least more substance than Arnold Toynbee's – and will survive longer. But it is unsettling to find a set of conclusions that follow from Slicher van Bath's calculations for cereal yields per grain sown in various West and East European coutries from 1250 to 1699, or F. Spooner's thoughts on diets, calculated in calories at various times and places in Western Europe, from the Spanish expedition to Morocco in 1578.[10] Braudel has assembled an ingenious but patchy collection of isolated figures - a* 'Mulhall's *Dictionary*' with a brain. *Les Structures du Quotidien* is a good read, lavishly illustrated. Yet it cannot be said to be a serious or successful attempt, with capitalism as a guide, to solve those 'basic problems and realities':

the long-term (*la longue durée*); divisions of economic life; world economies; secular trends and other fluctuations; the complex and complicating tangles of social hierarchies, not to say the class struggle; the ever-present yet varying role played by dominant minorities; even the series of industrial revolutions.[11]

ARGHIRI EMMANUEL

Emmanuel's *Unequal Exchange: a Study of the Imperialism of Trade* was published first in France in 1969. Emmanuel was engaged in a battle with economic doctrine and the theory of comparative costs in foreign trade. He 'refutes' the theory where lesser scholars – Maurice Bloch, Vilfredo Pareto, Bertil Ohlin – have failed.

My interest, as always, is in Emmanuel's sources rather than his argument. Can he *refute* a theory when his own figures are inadequate or even plain wrong? In establishing, for example, the differential between European and United States wage rates and the widening of the gap, his sources were *Cairnes, followed, from 1900, by the figures prepared by the International Labour Office in Geneva. If Cairnes's arguments were to be projected further to the present day, said Emmanuel, the gap between U S wages and those of 'certain countries in Asia, in Africa, in the Middle East, or in Latin America', would be 20 to 40 fold.[12]

'Certain countries . . . 20 to 40 fold' is not the language of science, or even of 'social' science; quite evidently the gap exists and can be established without such mathematics. But how useful is Cairnes for demonstrating the *history* of the phenomenon? John Elliot Cairnes (1823–1875) was a leading economist in his day, although not much of a writer (except as a contributor to the *Fortnightly Review*). Among his contemporaries he was valued for his explanation of the wages fund theory. Cairnes was a friend and follower of John Stuart Mill, a firm associate of the 'orthodox' school of economists, and a wholehearted supporter of *laissez-faire* and free trade. In the Victorian tradition, Cairnes never explained his sources, and his *Leading Principles* were in fact a dated remodelling of Smith, Malthus, Ricardo and Mill.

It is the quality that matters. Cairnes is a peculiar source for Marxist 'development history'. Emmanuel must have found so frail an authority convenient, and ignored his credentials, just as *Gunder Frank had entrusted his argument to an obscure Chilean 'historian',

Aníbal Pinto.[13] Emmanuel's indignant comparison of modern wage differentials with the absence (he claimed) of any differential whatsoever up to the third quarter of the nineteenth century, has some unlikely antecedents. By way of W. S. Jevons's *Theory of Political Economy* (1871) Emmanuel discovered that 'real wages in Classical Greece (328 BC) were not very different from those of unskilled workers in the nineteenth century'. Emmanuel, naturally, had not read Jevons in the original, but he was reassured by his source for the Jevons quotation. It was *Colin Clark, *The Conditions of Economic Progress*, who

> himself finds that the average income of the working class in Justinian's time was even higher than that in the Greece of the 1940's or in many other countries of South Eastern Europe, and equal to that in Great Britian in the 1850's or in Germany and France in the 1870's.[14]

Great thoughts and huge equations followed. Yet it is obvious that Emmanuel's *Unequal Exchange*, in the tradition of 'development history' with its massive (and eccentric) footnotes and bibliography, its fierce vocabulary and uncertain approach to sources, was engaged merely in political polemic. Emmanuel's argument for 'an incomes policy on the international scale corresponding to what exists, however imperfectly, inside the nation', was built on, among others, *Herbert Feis.[15] Revolution is Emmanuel's answer, and the overthrow of the capitalist system.[16]

IMMANUEL WALLERSTEIN

Immanuel Wallerstein, Director of the Fernand Braudel Center for the Study of Economies, Historical Systems and Civilizations (State University of New York at Binghamton), is a sociologist, formerly an Africanist, who has turned his attention to the history of the world economy since the sixteenth century. Wallerstein's distinctive contribution, it seems, is his 'famous world system perspective'. Albert Bergesen, also a sociologist, described the 'explosion of interest and research on this topic' ever since the first volume of Wallerstein's *Modern World System* was published in 1974, the hallmark of which was 'the broader view – large-scale, long-term social change'.[17] Bergesen, editor of a *Festschrift*, himself contributed a paper in which he identified the 'Long Waves of Colonial Expansion and Contraction, 1415–1969'. His researches included an 'extrapolation of some long-term trends of the world system since 1500', and he was able to add a helpful appendix which, although giving no indication of size, showed the 'Number of Colonies Established and Terminated Each Year and the Cumulative Net Number, 1415–1969'.[18] Bergesen's book ended with a traditionally extravagant bibliography that included *Time* magazine's interview of Deng Xiaoping in the issue for 5 February 1979.

Wallerstein admits disarmingly that he was trained as a social scientist and is still a professor of sociology, even if he had come to be regarded by some as having written a book (*The Modern World System*) about economic history. Nonetheless, he defends the role of what he calls 'historical social science', and concludes that 'truth becomes an interpretation, meaningful for our times, of the social world as it was, as it is, as it will be'.[19]

It is an ambitious enterprise: 'the rise and future demise of the world capitalist system'. The first volume of Wallerstein's *pensées* (New York, 1974) bears the full title *The Modern World System: Capitalist Agriculture and the Origins of the European World Economy in the Sixteenth Century*. Volume II (1980) is sub-titled *Mercantilism and the Consolidation of the European World Economy, 1600–1750*. Both volumes avoid quantification, although furnished with massive footnotes and vast bibliographies.

The Capitalist World Economy, a collection of eighteen Wallerstein papers, published by Cambridge in 1979, gave some indication of what is to come. It was part of a series, 'Studies in Modern Capitalism', 'devoted to an attempt to comprehend capitalism as a world system'. *The Capitalist World Economy*, like *The Modern World System*, is innocent of statistics – a sensible restraint, until more solid ground is reached.

SAMIR AMIN

Amin, a Marxist in the same tradition as Emmanuel (writing in French and publishing first in Paris), is not a great man for numbers. Perhaps, like Zdeněck Mlynář, he found at an early age that 'having mastered the very laws that govern the development of mankind and the world' (Marxist-Leninism) further research was now redundant since 'almost overnight [you become] a superior being with the correct views'.[20] Amin's *Unequal Development: An Essay on the Social Formations of Peripheral Capitalism* (New York, translation 1976) was not footnoted at all. His *Accumulation on a World Scale: A Critique of the Theory of Underdevelopment*, published by the Monthly Review Press a couple of years earlier, had at least included a bibliography peppered with the names of New York's veteran Hard Left – P. A. Baran, Harry Magdoff and Paul Sweezy. Amin's *Accumulation on a World Scale*, short as it was on references and figures, contained some tables that gave clues to his sources. Table 8, for example, presenting the 'ratio of prices of raw materials to prices of manufacturers and world trade', took the first half of its figures, for 1876–80 and 1881–85, from the *United Nations and *Imlah.

Amin's grasp of figures is better than *Wallerstein's. The difficulty with 'development historians' generally is that their *longue durée* is so enormous that they feel compelled to lunge at fragments of 'data', but have neither the time nor the specialist knowledge to evaluate them. Much use is made, necessarily, of the *League of Nations, the *United Nations, the *Royal Institute of International Affairs and *OECD, while all the familiar names recur: J. A. and *C. K. Hobson, *Jenks, *Feis, *Lewis, *Myrdal and *Nurkse. Amin's bibliography is almost as long as Wallerstein's. In neither case is there evidence of selectivity and discrimination.

ANDRÉ GUNDER FRANK

I am left with André Gunder Frank, from whom a great stream of 'development history' has emerged over the last twenty years. Frank's *Dependent Accumulation and Underdevelopment* (1978) is one of many, but it serves as well as another to illustrate Frank's 'method'.

Dependent Accumulation and Underdevelopment was 'an attempt to approach an explanation of underdevelopment through the analysis of the production and exchange relations of dependence within the world process of capital accumulation'. Supposedly it is a work of history, although written, like others of the same species, in a mood of high moral indignation. Its magpie technique – the collection of every kind and quality of figures, notions and facts – is again characteristic. When Frank reached 'world' trade – 'Patterns of World Trade Imbalances' – he made use of *Folke Hilgerdt/League of Nations. Hilgerdt again is to be found for Frank's Table 6 ('Merchandise Import and Export Balances, selected countries and years 1881–1913'), as he is for Table 3 ('Excess Exports and Imports, Europe and USA, 1881–1913'). Hilgerdt's figures were simply those of Western Europe and the United States, and to that extent Frank was treading on relatively safe ground. But he then used *Lamartine Yates to complete a more ambitious Table 7 from which, Frank expected, we would learn the exports and imports of Europe, North America, the less-developed world (Asia, Africa and Latin America) and Oceania, from 1876 to 1913!

The numerical base of Frank's *World Accumulation*, the prelude to *Dependent Accumulation and Underdevelopment*, defies description. It is in this book that Frank explains his own 'perspective' to be that of Marx's 'twelfth thesis on Feuerbach – the point is not simply to interpret the world, but to change it'.[21] The implications are unpleasant – 'world revolution', no less – and we would be unwise to ignore them.

CONCLUSION

Braudel's *longue durée* has fallen into strange hands. The *longue durée* and 'the long run/view' were respectable approaches to world history, however impracticable. 'Development history', in its preoccupation with 'unequal exchange' and the economic development of the periphery, delivers a political message for which the existence of solid evidence is immaterial. In a less heated atmosphere the shortage of numbers might simply have reflected an understandable reluctance to use bad numbers – a preference (like Braudel's) for wide reading and common sense. But what it really means, as we can see from the rare statistics that actually surface, is a lack of awareness either of the statistics that do exist or of the differences in quality they represent. Accuracy is not the point; it is the Message that counts. Keats spoke approvingly of 'Negative Capability', by which he meant the state 'when a man is capable of being in uncertainties, mysteries and doubts without irritable reaching after fact and reason'. His example was Coleridge, but 'development historians' (had he known them) would have served as well.

'World' history over the *longue durée* is no single anachronistic derivation from an interesting, but unprofessional, idea. E. L. Jones remarks the 'renewed interest in universal and *very* long-term history'. Wholly professional himself, Professor Jones's more recent preoccupation with *'very* long-term development in Europe from about AD 1400 to 1800', and comparisons with Asia, lead him into uncertain territory. Among the thirty or so authors he regards as 'central to the whole exercise' (*very* long-term history) is, of course, *Fernand Braudel, but also *D. C. North and R. P. Thomas, W. W. Rostow and *Immanuel Wallerstein.[22]

Notes

1. Robert William Fogel and G. R. Elton, *Which Road to the Past: Two Views of History* (New Haven, Conn., 1983) pp. 75, 110.
2. Simon Kuznets, *Economic Growth of Nations: Total Output and Production Structure* (Cambridge, Mass., 1971) p. 349.
3. Fernand Braudel, 'History and the Social Sciences: The Longue Durée', *Annales*, 4 (October/December 1958), republished in translation in *idem.*, *On History* (Chicago, 1980) p. 29.
4. *Ibid.*, p. 51.
5. Braudel, *Civilization and Capitalism, 15th–18th Century*, Vol. I. (London, 1981) p. 559.
6. *Ibid.*, p. 46.
7. *Ibid.*, p. 51.
8. *Ibid.*, p. 567, fn. 54.
9. *Ibid.*, pp. 58–9, 62.
10. *Ibid.*, pp. 124, 130–1.
11. *Ibid.*, Vol. III, p. 619.
12. Arghiri Emmanuel, *Unequal Exchange: A Study of the Imperialism of Trade* (trans. New York, 1972) p. 47.
13. André Gunder Frank, *Capitalism and Underdevelopment in Latin America: Historical Studies in Chile and Brazil* (New York, 1967).
14. Emmanuel, *Unequal Exchange*, p. 51.
15. *Ibid.*, p. 72.
16. *Ibid.*, p. 270.
17. Preface to Albert Bergesen (ed.), *Studies of the Modern World System* (New York, 1980) p. xiii.
18. Bergesen, *Modern World System*, pp. 271, 273–5.
19. Immanuel Wallerstein, 'Some Reflections on History, the Social Sciences and Politics', in Wallerstein, *The Capitalist World-Economy* (Cambridge, 1979) p. xii.
20. Zdeněk Mlynář, *Night Frost in Prague: The End of Humane Socialism* (London, 1980) pp. 2–3.

21. André Gunder Frank, *World Accumulation, 1492–1789* (New York, 1978) p. 22.
22. E. L. Jones, *The European Miracle: Environments, Economies, and Geopolitics in the History of Europe and Asia* (Cambridge, 1981) pp. 249–50.

Conclusion

Who, these days, can find profit from more than the odd detail in *Michael Mulhall? – yet they claim to have done so. Who, not so long ago, recommended *Kuznets, *Myrdal, *Ohlin and *Lewis for the Nobel Prize in Economics ? – yet they did. Who, even now, can take seriously the 'Balance of Payments' calculations of *C. K. Hobson and *Albert Imlah? – yet they most certainly do. I have already explained that I cannot myself offer substitute figures other than those that I have calculated for Britain's investment abroad, 1815–1914, and Hilaire Belloc's advice may have some point: 'always keep a hold on Nurse', he warned, 'for fear of finding something worse.' But I can (and should) call attention to points of interest and weakness, in the hope that some of the conventional conclusions will now be re-drawn. 'In *good* traditional history, as in *good* scientific history,' Sir Geoffrey Elton explains, 'the quality of the work or sources alone decides the quality and the acceptability of the history written.'[1]

The distinction is confused, without doubt, by those disingenuous compliments so liberally distributed throughout the literature. Praise heaped on an earlier authority spares further investigation. It is so characteristic of 'world' history that it must surely be acknowledged for what it normally is – the evasion of an awkward question.

*Taussig (1927) found the Victorian statistician, A. L. Rowley, to be 'an observer whose competence is not to be questioned'.[2] The *United Nations (1951) based its long-range population estimates for 1650 to 1900 primarily on the 'careful research' of *Walter F. Willcox (1930s).[3] *Sir Arthur Lewis (1952) was dependent for 'world' statistics on the 'magnificent work done by the *League of Nations' (1945).[4] *Ragnar Nurkse (1953) found the identical volume (Hilgerdt's *Industrialization and Foreign Trade*, Geneva, 1945) an 'illuminating study,'[5] while *Sir Alexander Cairncross (1955) praised the 'pioneer work' of *Hilgerdt and proceeded to use it without further comment.[6] When delivering the Wicksell Lectures, *Ragnar Nurkse (1959) referred further to the 'carefully revised' volume indices in *Albert Imlah's *Economic Elements in the Pax Britannica* (1958).[7] *Angus Maddison (1962) praised *von Neumann-Spallart (1881) for having written a 'pioneer world economic survey'.[8] *Arghiri Emmanuel (1969) was pleased to use the 'concise figures given by *H. Feis' (1930).[9] *Maddison (1971) later discovered *Zimmerman (1962) to be 'an immensely valuable summary of information on national incomes in the Third World during the nineteenth century'.[10] Jeffrey Nugent (1973) praised *Imlah's 'careful study' on Britain's terms of trade (1959).[11] Walter Rostow (1978) did not conceal his unease at linking *Mulhall to *Hilgerdt, but he consoled himself with the thought that one could always rely on Mulhall's 'rather high and demonstrated record for good sense and judgement'.[12]

Methinks they do protest too much. *John R. Hanson II (1980) made a point of praising famous men. *Paul Lamartine Yates's *Forty Years of Foreign Trade* (1969) was, to Hanson, 'a respected statistical survey of LDC [less developed country] trade between 1913 and 1953', but he also admired the 'excellent statistical compendia supplied by international agencies during both the interwar and postwar periods'. He was delighted by the 'meticulously presented' data of the *Statistical Abstract of Foreign Countries* published (in 1909) by the US Department of Commerce. But then he discovered those 'remarkable' compendia of foreign statistics gathered and published by Britain's Board of Trade from the 1830s, quite apart from *Macgregor's *Commercial Statistics*.[13] And *Bairoch's 'exhaustive analysis of trends in the volume and value of European exports' came in for its measure of praise.[14]

The weaker the source, the louder the praise. When *Maddison (1982) collected his GDP calculations from 'substantial statistical research by distinguished scholars', he might have heeded Gunnar Myrdal's advice. Most of the figures employed uncritically in attempts to analyse growth and development in underdeveloped countries, said Myrdal, are 'not only statistically weak in the ordinary sense but grossly misconceived'. Myrdal was sure that the 'now commonly compiled figures for GNP or national income are not worthy of remaining the kingpin of that analysis'.[15]

Long waves (Kuznets) or the *longue durée* (Braudel) are indeed complicated, and Kondratieff's three great cycles in the movement of the price level between the end of the 1780s and the 1920s have attracted more attention than they deserve.[16] *Lewis wondered whether we should not be talking about 'an eighteen year cycle, with peaks in 1872, 1889 and 1907, superimposed upon a deep Kondratieff swing'. Yet even *Lewis (1952) thought that it might be premature to talk of long cycles in advance of further investigation.[17] *Braudel had no such doubts, and he put cyclical movement 'in the forefront of research'.[18] Yet to *Jacob Viner, a skilled economist and economic historian, it was 'purely fantastic' to accept propositions like a norm of thirty-seven months for the duration of the business cycle, or an annual 3 per cent as the 'law' for the growth of capital.[19]

I am not denying that results *can* be achieved. There are whole areas where this is already the case, and it will surely become true for some at least of the more recondite aspects of global research. The preconditions are first a real knowledge of the area investigated (if only to check those results), and second, more generally, a strong streak of common sense. 'Upper-bound' and 'lower-bound' estimates are a sensible (and fashionable) approach to such uncertainties, but they are not the complete answer. Poor figures throughout, upper to lower, cannot be relied upon to produce a useful result.

Thirty years have passed since *Braudel, and sixty since *Viner. Even if ultimately we may come to accept Braudel's opinion that 'the "long view" must surely be the wise man's time span',[20] I hope that this book may at least have suggested that there is much ground to be covered before then. Meanwhile, 'whereof one cannot speak, thereon one must remain silent' (Ludwig Wittgenstein).

Notes

1. Robert Williams Fogel and G. R. Elton, *Which Road to the Past: Two Views of History* (New Haven, Conn., 1983) p. 106.
2. F. W. Taussig, *International Trade* (New York, 1927) p. 240.
3. United Nations, Department of Social Affairs: Population Division, *Population Bulletin*, No. 1 (New York, 1951) p. 2.
4. W. A. Lewis, 'World Production, Prices and Trade, 1870–1960,' *Manchester School of Economics and Social Studies*, XX:2 (May 1952) p. 105.
5. Ragnar Nurkse, *Problems of Capital Formation in Underdeveloped Countries* (Oxford, 1953) p. 21.
6. A. K. Cairncross, 'World Trade in Manufactures since 1900', *Economia Internazionale*, VIII (1955) pp. 715, 721.
7. Ragnar Nurkse, *Patterns of Trade and Development* (Stockholm, 1959) p. 20.
8. Angus Maddison, 'Growth and Fluctuation in the World Economy, 1870–1960', Banca Nazionale del Lavoro, *Quarterly Review*, XV:61 (1962) p. 168, fn. 20.

9. Arghiri Emmanuel, *Unequal Exchange: A Study of the Imperialism of Trade* (trans. New York, 1972) p. 45.
10. Maddison, *Class Structure and Economic Growth* (New York, 1971) pp. 22–3.
11. Jeffrey B. Nugent, 'Exchange-Rate Movements and Economic Development in the late Nineteenth Century', *Journal of Political Economy*, 81 (1973) p. 1116, fn. 1.
12. W. W. Rostow, *The World Economy: History and Prospect* (London, 1978) p. 659.
13. John R. Hanson II, *Trade and Transition: Exports from the Third World, 1840–1900* (New York, 1980) pp. 2, 8 and 9.
14. *Ibid.*, p. 15.
15. Gunnar Myrdal, *Against the Stream: Critical Essays on Economics* (trans. London, 1974) pp. 195–6.
16. N. D. Kondratieff, 'The Long Waves in Economic Life,' *Review of Economic Statistics*, XVII:6 (November, 1935, trans. from the original German of 1926).
17. W. A. Lewis, 'World Production, Prices and Trade,' p. 127.
18. Fernand Braudel, 'History and the Social Sciences: the Longue Durée', first published in *Annales* (1958), and subsequently in translation in Braudel's essays and reviews *On History* (Chicago, 1980) p. 27.
19. Jacob Viner, 'The Present Status and Future Prospects of Quantitative Economics', reprinted from the *American Economic Review*, Supplement, 18 (March 1928) in Viner, *The Long View and the Short: Studies in Economic Theory and Policy* (Glencoe, Illinois, 1958) p. 45.
20. Braudel, 'History and the Social Sciences', p. 48.

Index